# Rugby Union Laws
## EXPLAINED

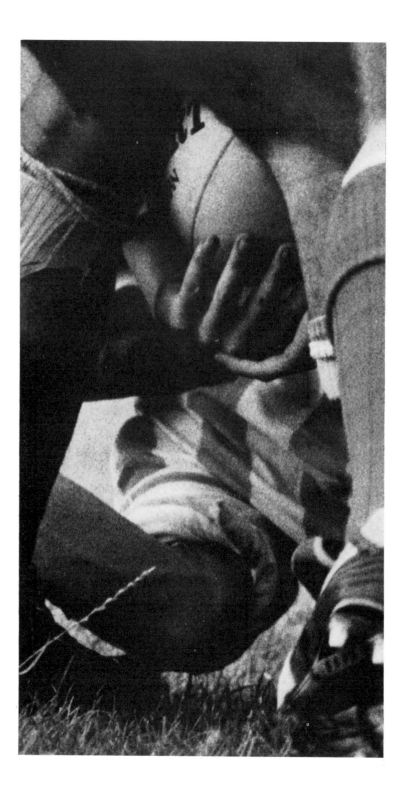

# *Rugby Union Laws*
# EXPLAINED

## Jim Fleming
## &
## Brian Anderson

Foreword by Bill McLaren

Lochar Publishing • Moffat • Scotland

Laws reprinted by kind permission of the International Rugby Football Board

© Jim Fleming & Brian Anderson, 1991

Published by Lochar Publishing Ltd
MOFFAT DG10 9ED

**British Library Cataloguing in Publication Data**
Fleming, Jim
 Rugby Union laws explained.
 1. Rugby Union Football
 I. Title  II. Anderson, Brian
 796.333

 ISBN 0-948403-62-4


Typeset in Garamond 49 on 10/13pt
by Chapterhouse, The Cloisters, Halsall Lane, Formby

**Book Designed** by Mark Blackadder

**Illustrations by** John Wilkinson

**Photographs** of referee's signals by David Harrold,
other photographs courtesy of *The Scotsman*


Printed in Great Britain by BPCC Wheatons Ltd, Exeter

# CONTENTS

# FOREWORD

Most of us at one time or another, either *sotto voce* or with a foghorn
bellow from the stand or terracing, have voiced criticisms of refereeing
decisions especially where they went against our favourite team. Some
criticism is just good-natured banter and that happens on as well as
off the field. A famous England fullback once became so exasperated
with the official in charge that he felt obliged to proffer advice as to
his implementation of law. Eventually, fed up with the barbs, the
referee snarled at his critic, 'Now, look here, who is refereeing this
game, you or me?'. The cutting retort was, 'With all due respect sir,
neither of us!'

That international player probably knew his laws fairly well even
though there are twenty-eight of them occupying some one hundred
and fifteen pages of the Scottish Rugby Union's laws handbook. But
much of the criticism directed at referees is ill-founded because many
supporters and, indeed, players, just are not conversant with the finer
points of law.

Referees deserve a better deal. They are a remarkable breed. It never
ceases to amaze me that they do a job with masochistic connotation
yet with admirable tact and good humour, accept all the flak with
good grace and keep going back for more. All this despite the fact
that their function has been rendered more difficult by the intense
pressure placed upon them and players by the highly-charged,
competitive element in virtually every grade of play that has
encouraged an all-consuming desire to win, almost at all costs. In
addition to all that, quite frequent law alterations with new wordings
have to be accommodated.

All of which surely points to the need for a simple way of grasping the
meaning of the various laws so that they will be understood easily by
rugby folk everywhere. Well, this is it! The authors and publishers of
this book have rendered the game a considerable service by explaining
the whys and wherefores of rugby law in an easily readable manner.
The game needs this kind of book and it was no surprise that the
publishers should turn to Brian Anderson and Jim Fleming to fulfil

the task. Each is a referee of vast experience and of World Cup stature. Each knows his laws backwards and has administered them with such a practised touch as to have earned the highest respect from players and fellow officials everywhere. Each is in love with the Rugby Union game and seeks to protect its image and reputation.

By this valuable work they surely have gone a long way towards broadening the readers' knowledge of the meaning and aim of Rugby Union law. Not that this will totally eradicate the kind of quip that every referee has to accept, for instance, on the occasion when a player in the darkened recesses of a maul commented that the referee was blind. When the referee asked, 'What was that you said?' the reply came back, 'Blimey, he's deaf as well'! Hopefully, through the influence of this book, players and supporters will become more enlightened about the wording and meaning of the law, those brave souls with the whistle will enjoy an easier passage and games too, will be subject to fewer stoppages and so will be far more enjoyable for players, referees and supporters alike.

BILL McLAREN

# INTRODUCTION

When asked to prepare this book we had to decide at which level we should pitch it. Accordingly, it was felt that, after printing the laws as they were written, we should put each law into simple English for the benefit of players, coaches, referees, supporters or whoever. We may reiterate certain points but this is intentional as it was felt the message in certain aspects of the game must be re-emphasised.

Although the book might appear to be directed mainly to those whose interests lie in refereeing, it should also assist everyone connected with rugby, including spectators, to understand the laws of the game. It will also help those thinking of taking up refereeing or serve as useful revision material for more experienced referees.

Without a referee, there would not be a game. One good reason for a knowledgeable referee is to allow thirty men, boys or ladies to enjoy a game of rugby. The game is for the players; the referee should always be No. 31 on the field of play.

Nevertheless, good referees are appreciated by players and spectators alike. And a good referee is one whose decisions are correct most of the time and whose manner and personality are acceptable to players and coaches both on and off the field of play. The referee who is not only knowledgeable, but is also fit, fair, firm yet sympathetic and has good communication, consistency and control will not go far wrong.

Once at the top as a referee, as in every walk of life, the perks of the job are there. We have been two of the 'lucky' few who have refereed in twenty different countries in five different continents.

If you do decide, or have already decided, or you have been 'volunteered' by club or school to take up refereeing, it is presumed that you will want to be as good a referee as you can be. The better you do, the more enjoyable it will be for the players and for you. To make progress, think about the laws, positioning and decision making. To gain experience, referee as often as you can and talk to your senior referees, those that are successful. One of the best places to do the latter is at the meetings of your local referees society.

There is much more to good refereeing than knowing the laws inside out, although that is important; it is equally important how a good referee applies the laws, which is one of the reasons we have enjoyed producing this book. Knowledge of the game and understanding of the laws helps everyone's enjoyment of rugby, both those participating on the field of play and those watching. An appreciation of what is going on has to be good for all concerned, and whether you be player, coach, referee, supporter or none of these we hope you enjoy the book – but above all else, enjoy this great game of ours.

## Notes

⌐ Indicates post with flag.

Length and breadth of field to be as near to dimensions indicated as possible. All areas to be rectangular.

The distance from the goal line to the dead-ball line should be not less than 10 metres where practicable.

– – – – These broken lines indicate 10 metres distance from the half-way line and 5 metres distance from the touch lines.

_____ These lines at the goal-lines and intersecting the 22 metres and 10 metres lines and the half-way line are 15 metres from the touch lines. The lines at the goal-lines extend 5 metres into the field-of-play.

Goal dimensions: 3.00 metres is taken from the ground to the top edge of the crossbar and 5.60 metres from inside to inside of the goal posts.

A minimum height of 1.20 metres above the ground is desirable for corner posts.

# LAW 1
## *The Plan*

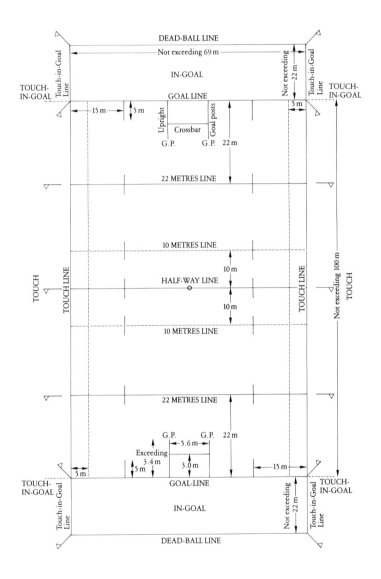

# LAW 1
## *Ground*

The field-of-play is the area as shown on the plan, bounded by, but not including, the goal lines and touch lines.

The *playing area* is the field-of-play and In-goal.

The *playing enclosure* is the playing area and a reasonable area surrounding it.

The *Plan*, including all words and figures thereon, is to take effect as part of these Laws.

The *Terms* appearing on the Plan are to bear their apparent meaning and to be deemed part of the definitions as if separately included.

1. All lines shown on the plan must be suitably marked out. The touch lines are in touch. The goal lines are in In-goal. The dead-ball line is *not* in In-goal. The touch-in-goal lines and corner posts are in touch-in-goal. The goal posts are to be erected in the goal lines. The twenty two metres lines are in the twenty two metres areas.

2. The game must be played on a ground of the area (maximum) shown on the plan and marked in accordance with the plan. The surface must be grass-covered or, where this is not available, clay or sand provided the surface is not of dangerous hardness.

3. Any objection by the visiting team about the ground or the way in which it is marked out must be made to the referee before the first kick-off.

## LAW 1

It should be noted that whilst there are maximum distances, there are no minimum requirements.

One of the games in the 1990 Italian World Cup Qualifying group was played in a soccer stadium with only a five metre In-goal area at each end of the pitch. At kick-off and all restart kicks, in a situation as this, it is vitally important that the touch judge away from the forwards is positioned near to the defending goal line. He is then in a position to help the referee in a long kick situation by signalling to him whether the ball has directly gone on or over the dead-ball line.

If this does happen, the receiving team can elect for the ball to be kicked off again, have a scrummage formed at the centre or accept the kick by electing to take a drop-out on their twenty two metre line.

In any event it is advisable for the referee to inspect the pitch as soon as possible after his arrival to check for any strange or incorrect markings.

# LAW 2
## *Ball*

1. The ball when new shall be oval in shape, of four panels and of the following dimensions-

| | |
|---|---|
| Length in line | 280 to 300 mm |
| Circumference (end on) | 760 to 790 mm |
| Circumference (in width) | 580 to 620 mm |
| Weight | 400 to 440 gms |

## LAW 2

The match balls used in any game are the same for both sides and should be checked before the game by at least one of the match officials. Most groundsmen are efficient at their job and know exactly what is required, but if the referee finds that the balls are rock hard or too soft, there should be someone on hand from the home club to make any necessary adjustment.

Some referees carry pressure gauges around with them to ensure the correct pressure. However, these are ineffective unless the exact level of the pitch above sea level is known.

# LAW 3
## *Number of Players*

1. A match shall be played by not more than fifteen players in each team.

2. When a Union authorises matches to be played with fewer than fifteen players, the Laws of the Game shall apply except that there will be no fewer than three players in a scrummage at all times.

3. Replacement of players shall be allowed in recognised trial matches as determined by the Union having jurisdiction over the match.

4. In all other matches, a player may be replaced only on account of injury and subject to the following conditions:
   a. Not more than three players in each team may be replaced.
   **Exceptions:**
   Up to six players may be replaced:
      i.   in matches between teams of schoolboys or teams where all players are under the age of twenty-one, the age limitation being applied from the commencement of the official season of the visited Union.
      ii.   in domestic matches as determined by the Union having jurisdiction over the match.
   b. A player who has been replaced must *not* resume playing in the match.

5. a. In matches in which a national representative team is playing, a player may be replaced *only* when, in the opinion of a medical practitioner, the player is so injured that he should not continue playing in the match.
   b. For such competition and other domestic matches as a Union gives express permission, an injured player may be replaced:
   — on the advice of a medically trained person, or
   — if a medically trained person is not present, with the approval of the referee.

6. If the referee is advised by a doctor or other medically trained

person or for any other reason considers that a player is so injured that it would be harmful for him to continue playing, the referee shall require the player to leave the playing area. For this purpose the referee may also require a player to leave the field to be examined medically.

7. Any objection by either team as regards the number of players in a team may be made to the referee at any time but objections shall not affect any score previously obtained.

# LAW 3

Whilst most players who are injured accept medical advice and retire to be replaced, there have been occasions when this has not been the case.

Take a front-row forward with a head cut who does not think the cut is severe although it is bleeding. In this case paragraph 6 would come into operation, because not only could it be harmful for him to continue playing, it could also be harmful for others. He must leave the field to get the cut either bandaged or stitched as required and if he doesn't leave of his own free will then the referee is perfectly entitled to send him off.

# LAW 4
## *Players' Dress*

1. A player must not wear dangerous projections such as buckles or rings.

2. Shoulder pads of the 'harness' type must not be worn. If the referee is satisfied that a player requires protection following an injury to a shoulder, the wearing of a pad of cottonwool, sponge rubber or similar soft material may be permitted provided the pad is attached to the body or sewn on to the jersey.

3. Studs of a player's boots must conform to the British Standard BS 6366: 1983. They must be circular, securely fastened to the boots and of the following dimensions:

   Maximum length
   (measured from sole)                              18 mm
   Minimum diameter at base                          13 mm
   Minimum diameter at top                           10 mm
   Minimum diameter of integral washer               20 mm

   The wearing of a single stud at the toe of the boot is prohibited.
   **Note**
   The moulded rubber multi-studded sole is acceptable under this Law.

4. The referee has power to decide before or during the match that any part of a player's dress is dangerous. He must then order the player to remove the dangerous part and permit him to resume playing in the match only after it has been removed.

## LAW 4

Where a player has a shoulder injury prior to the match and a shoulder pad has been advised by a medical practitioner, then the doctor's line authorising the wearing of it should be produced to the referee prior to the game. This will then avoid any recrimination after the game by the opposition, provided the pad is attached to the body or sewn on to the jersey.

The checking of studs prior to the game and every pair of boots, including replacements should be checked to ensure they are the correct size (by checking them against the stud gauge) and that each stud carries the relevant 'kite' mark.

When arriving at the ground a considerate referee will check with each coach to find out the most convenient time for his side to have their boots checked. The last thing he wants is a referee coming into the dressing room five minutes before kick-off to check studs.

If both teams want their boots checked at approximately the same time – fine as both captains will be there – after the stud check is an ideal time to 'toss-up'.

# LAW 5
## *Toss, Time*

**No-side is the end of a match.**

1. Before a match begins the captains shall toss for the right to kick-off or the choice of ends.

2. The duration of play in a match shall be such time not exceeding eighty minutes as shall be directed by the Union or, in the absence of such direction, as agreed upon by the teams or, if not agreed, as fixed by the referee. In International matches two periods of forty minutes each shall be played.

3. Play shall be divided into two halves. At half-time the teams shall change ends and there shall be an interval of not more than five minutes.

4. A period not exceeding one minute shall be allowed for treatment of an injury to a player or for any other permitted delay. A longer period may be allowed only if the additional time is required for the removal of an injured player from the playing area.

   Playing time lost as a result of any such permitted delay or of delay in taking a kick at goal shall be made up in that half of the match in which the delay occurred, subject to he power vested in the referee to declare no-side before time has expired.

# LAW 5

As with checking studs it is helpful to find out what is the most convenient time to toss for each side. Most sides are happy to toss ten minutes before kick-off but if the toss is to be done earlier and the sides cannot agree then it is up to the referee to determine when the toss will take place. The side winning the toss has the option to take the kick or choose the direction the team will play. On winning the toss some captains state – 'we will decide on the pitch'. Is this an unfair advantage to the toss winning team? Some say yes, because for the last, very important ten minutes before kick-off one side knows exactly what it is going to do, eg – kick deep, play with the wind, play into the sun, . . . while the other side are left in the dark. If the toss-losing captain at the toss states he wants to have a decision at the toss up then it would seem fair to ask the winning captain what he is going to do.

Now that injured players can be treated for injury while play continues, there are not as many stoppages as in the past. A good referee will be aware that a player is being treated and will look for a signal that if the injury is serious, play should be stopped. Only then should he stop his watch – but he must remember to restart it as soon as play recommences. If a player has gone off, then for the next few minutes he should keep half an eye on the tunnel for the replacement. Of course if the play moves towards and in close proximity to the player who is being attended to, a good referee will stop play to avoid a collision and award a scrum to the side in possession of the ball.

The referee must make up time lost through any delay in taking a kick at goal in each half. This applies whether or not the referee considers the undue delay to be that of the kicker or any other member of his team. Playing time lost should begin from forty seconds after the player has indicated his intention to kick at goal. If after a further minute the kick has still not been taken then the referee should award a scrummage at the point of penalty with the original penalised side putting the ball in.

# LAW 6
## *Referee and Touch Judges*

### A.  REFEREE

1.  There shall be a referee for every match. He shall be appointed by or under the authority of the Union or, in case no such authorised referee has been appointed, a referee may be mutually agreed upon between the teams or, failing such agreement, he shall be appointed by the home team.

2.  If the referee is unable to officiate for the whole period of a match a replacement shall be appointed either in such manner as may be directed by the Union or, in the absence of such direction, by the referee or, if he is unable to do so, by the home team.

3.  The referee shall keep the time and the score, and he must in every match apply fairly the Laws of the Game without any variation or omission, except only when the Union has authorised the application of an experimental law approved by the International Board.

4.  He must not give any instruction or advice to either team prior to the match. During the match he must not consult with anyone except:
    a. either or both touch judges on a point of fact relevant to their functions, or on matters relating to Law 26(3), or
    b. in regard to time.

5.  The referee is the sole judge of fact and of law. All his decisions are binding on the players. He cannot alter a decision except when given before he observes that a touch judge's flag is raised or before he receives a report related to Law 26(3) from a touch judge.

6.  The referee must carry a whistle and must blow it:
    a. to indicate the beginning of the match, half-time, resumption of play after half-time, no-side, a score of a touch-down, and
    b. to stop play because of infringement or otherwise as required by the Laws.

7. During a match no person other than the players, the referee and the touch judges may be within the playing enclosure or the playing area unless with the permission of the referee which shall be given only for a special and temporary purpose.

Play may continue during minor injuries with a medically trained person being permitted to come on to the playing area to attend the player or the player going to the touch line.

Continuation of playing during minor injuries is subject to the referee's permission and to his authority to stop play at any time.

8. a. All players must respect the authority of the referee and they must not dispute his decisions. They must (except in the case of a kick-off) stop playing at once when the referee has blown his whistle.

b. A player must when so requested, whether before or during the match, allow the referee to inspect his dress.

c. A player must not leave the playing enclosure without the referee's permission. If a player retires during a match because of injury or otherwise, he must not resume playing in that match until the referee has given him permission.

# LAW 6
## *Refereeing philosophy*

While it is practically impossible to develop a complete uniformity of refereeing, there are certain characteristics of refereeing that should be common to all referees. Refereeing exchanges between countries and hemispheres have attempted to achieve this uniformity, and there are certain characteristics which help a good referee to become a better one.

*Unobtrusive but firm*
It is paramount that the referee perceives himself as the thirty

first person on the field. His on-the-field demeanour should be low key, not laid back, while he assists the games progress within the framework of the laws. He must be firm to maintain control but not over officious.

The referee must have a positive approach to the game. The referee's job is to control matters from the beginning so that the players know exactly what is required of them. The referee must do this in such a manner that he gets the players 'on his side'. There is no point in starting a match with a 'them and us' scenario, and it is essential that the referee and players get on the same wavelength as soon as possible. The referee can try and achieve this by speaking to the players and telling them exactly what he wants. It is essential that he does not attempt this in a dictatorial manner. It is often said that a referee should 'set out his stall' early. This means that he should let the players know by word and action how, for instance, he wants the scrum to form, the line-out to stand and how he will play the off-side law. This should *not* be carried out by shouting at players, talking down to them or a general waving about of hands.

A good referee will always err on the constructive side rather than the destructive side as long as the law is being complied with. He should always allow a little longer in certain circumstances to allow the ball to be played in order that the game is kept fluid.

*Correctness in law*
It should be the goal of every referee to officiate games consistently without making errors in law. All referees make errors in judgement, but good referees should never make errors in actual law. To attain this correctness in law it is obvious that the referee must know the law book from front to back cover, from the obvious infringement to the more obscure which might only happen once in his refereeing career. However, while striving to become correct in law, the referee should avoid becoming pedantic. The law book designates

degrees of offences by making them major or minor infringements. The referee must see that the laws are obeyed with the minimum use of sanctions. But once having set his course he must pursue it to its logical conclusion. If, for instance, he has penalised a hooker twice for striking the ball too early, it is fatal and quite wrong to overlook the next time the hooker does it, because he feels reluctant to give further penalties.

*Fairness*

Fairness is synonymous with consistency. As was stated earlier, players want to know how the referee will apply the laws during that specific game. Players are aware that no two referees will apply the laws identically. Therefore, during the course of a game, the players want the referee to apply the laws in a consistent manner to both teams.

It is essential that if he makes a mistake during a game which is obvious to the players, a good referee will apologise. If he does not, players might assume that the referee does not know that particular law and take the law into their own hands.

Similarly, if a referee makes a mistake or an error of judgement, he should not under any circumstance try and 'even the score up' at the next infringement by either ignoring an infringement or by giving an unfair advantage to the wronged team.

The referee should always try to provide an explanation if the law is applied in a way which perhaps the players were not expecting or anticipating. Players usually will accept a referee's shortcomings so long as he is fair and consistent in what he does throughout a game. It quite often happens that a referee notices an infringement but for one reason or another does not penalise, perhaps because of the advantage law. It is a good idea to take the opportunity at the next suitable situation to explain quietly and unobstrusively in order to let the player or players concerned know that the offence was in fact seen.

Also in order to be fair it is essential that a referee does not refer to players on the field by their first names. There is no way that a referee will know the first names of all the players therefore if he refers to some by name and not others, players might think he favours certain players.

*Fitness*
It should not be necessary to emphasise the importance of fitness. A fit referee may not be a good referee but a quality referee is always fit. Lack of fitness reflects a lack of respect for the players. Players train to improve their fitness so why should the referee not do likewise? The same principles apply to degrees of fitness. Higher standards of games require higher standards of fitness. In general referees tend to make more errors in judgement and law when they are tired.

*Preventative refereeing*
Mention has been made earlier that the ideal referee should be unobtrusive and should not be pedantic. The referee should not be on the field primarily to catch the players breaking the law, although that is part and parcel of his function, but rather he should be on the field to try and encourage the players to play the game within the laws. Obviously a lot also depends on the players actions. If players are intent on breaking the laws, the referee has no option but to hand out penalty after penalty.

A lot of circumstances can be prevented by word rather than incessant whistle. Technical offences can be corrected by the referee speaking to players in the first instance rather than waiting for the infringement to take place and then awarding a penalty. For instance, a good referee will, at the first few scrums, tell the scrum halves to put the ball in straight. Hopefully, the players will accept the advice and no free kick will have to be awarded. A bad referee will not speak to the player, will wait until the ball has not been put in straight and award the free kick. Referees must be careful that the advice or warnings that they impart to the players does not become a form of coaching, which is of course, contrary to law.

*Concentration and control*

In order to referee well, a referee must concentrate throughout the game. He must give his full and undivided attention to the game. It is easy to be distracted by spectators, especially if they are few and close to the touch line. It is important that referees switch off as far as possible where spectators are concerned. Under no circumstances should a referee answer back any comment that has been made in his direction by a spectator. By concentrating in a game a good referee will be able to read the game and anticipate what is going to be done by the players. It is essential that the referee get himself involved in the tactics of the game.

As we touched on earlier, consistency in a referee is essential. One of the greatest criticisms that could be levelled at a referee by players, coaches or spectators is that he is inconsistent. It is most annoying during a game if one team is habitually penalised for killing the ball while the other is not. It is not that the referee is biased, although this cannot be ruled out, rather he is being inconsistent in interpretation.

*Positioning*

In order to make the correct decisions, apart from being fit and up with play, a referee must be in a position from which he can see clearly what has happened, while at the same time he must not obstruct players in any way. It is obvious that in some situations there is no single correct position and in others, no matter where the referee is, he will not be able to see everything. Likewise, a tall referee might take up different positions, because of his height, than a smaller referee would.

No matter what position a referee takes up, he must feel comfortable in himself, see as much as possible, not interfere with the players and keep moving. A static referee is a poor referee. A good referee should always keep moving and be alert to what is or might be happening.

*Referee signals*

Signalling by referees has always produced discussion as to necessity and for whom the signals are intended. Indeed there are only four signals which a referee is obliged to give during a game. These are to signal a penalty kick, to signal a free kick or mark, when a try or penalty try has been awarded and to indicate which side has the put-in to a scrummage. Thereafter, it is left entirely to the referee whether he signals or not.

In order to make the game more understandable it is helpful if a referee can give some indication to players, spectators and media men the nature of any particular offence.

We hope that the following signals and accompanying explanations, which are generally used by referees, will give some indication and understanding to people as to the nature of certain offences. It should be noted however that, apart from the signals already noted, none of these signals are mandatory, neither is the list exhaustive.

PENALTY KICK:- Arm raised at an angle of approx 60 degrees pointing to the side of the non-offending team.

FREE KICK:- Forearm raised vertically with upper arm horizontal. The arm should be pointing towards the team who have been awarded the free kick.

TRY OR PENALTY TRY:- Arm fully extended upwards. The referee should be as close to the mark of the try as possible, facing towards the half way line.

SCRUMMAGE AWARD:- Facing the mark of the scrummage, forearm horizontal pointing to the side who are to put the ball in.

FORWARD PASS OR THROW FORWARD:- Passing gesture in the general direction of the forward pass or throw forward.

KNOCK ON:- One hand above the head being tapped by the other hand.

NOT RELEASING THE BALL QUICKLY ENOUGH:- Arms folded across the chest as if holding the ball.

FALLING ON OR OVER A PLAYER ON THE GROUND:- Arched arm gesturing a movement towards the ground.

PULLING THE SCRUMMAGE DOWN:- Clenched fist with bent arm making a pulling down gesture.

WHEELING SCRUMMAGE ILLEGALLY:- Clenched fist with bent arm making a pulling gesture.

SCRUM WHEELING MORE THAN 90 DEGREES OR OFFSIDE AT RUCK / MAUL:- Rotating index finger pointing towards the ground.

FOOT UP AT SCRUMMAGE:- Touching raised foot with hand.

SCRUMMAGE PUT IN NOT STRAIGHT:- Two hands indicating direction of ball into scrummage.

WILFULLY COLLAPSING RUCK OR MAUL:- Arms and upper body moving in a downwards direction as if pulling an opponent to the ground.

ILLEGAL HANDLING ON THE GROUND IN SCRUM, RUCK OR AFTER A TACKLE:- Hand making a sweeping movement at ground level.

BARGING IN LINE OUT:- Bent arm at right angles to body, barging movement of arm away from body.

JUMPING OFF SHOULDERS OR LEVERING IN LINE OUT:- Bent arm, downward movement of arm.

PUSHING IN LINE OUT:- Arms at shoulder height, palms open with pushing gesture.

LIFTING AT LINE OUT:- Fists clenched, lifting gesture from waist upwards.

CLOSING GAPS IN THE LINE OUT:- Palms of hands facing each other at head height making a 'squeezing' movement.

NOT STRAIGHT AT THE LINE OUT:- Movement of hand above the head indicating the line of the ball.

OFFSIDE AT SCRUM, RUCK OR MAUL (IN FRONT OF REAR FOOT):- Straight arm behind back, swinging back and forwards signifying position of offside line.

OBSTRUCTION IN GENERAL PLAY:- Forearms crossed and then uncrossed in front of chest indicating a crossing movement by players.

OFFSIDE (OPTIONAL PENALTY OR SCRUM BACK):- One arm raised as for a penalty kick, the other pointing back towards the position of the scrum. After the selection is made, the appropriate signal is made at the selected position.

OFFSIDE (REMAINING WITHIN 10 METRES):- Rotating hand in circle above head, other hand indicating offside player.

HIGH OR DANGEROUS TACKLE:- Movement of hand across front of neck.

ILLEGAL USE OF THE BOOT:- Downward stamping gesture of boot.

ILLEGAL PUNCHING:- Open hand punched by clenched fist.

ADVANTAGE:- One arm outstretched at waist height pointing towards the non-offending team. The arm will be taken down once the referee has deemed a team has gained sufficient advantage.

DISSENT BY A PLAYER:- Arm outstretched, hand mimicking a talking movement.

FORMATION OF A SCRUMMAGE:- Arms bent above head with hands touching.

ACCIDENTALLY OFFSIDE:- Clenched fists in front of chest making a 'squeezing' movement.

BALL HELD UP OVER GOAL LINE:- Open palms facing each other vertically, indicating the height the ball was above the ground.

PLAYER ILLEGALLY LYING ON THE GROUND:- Forearms in front of chest making a rotating movement indicating player not rolling or moving away from the ball.

'STAY ON YOUR FEET':- Open palms of hands facing upwards together with an upward movement from the waist.

# LAW 6
## *Referee and Touch Judges*

### B.   TOUCH JUDGES

1.  There shall be two touch judges for every match. Unless touch judges have been appointed by or under the authority of the Union, it shall be the responsibility of each team to provide a touch judge.

2.  A touch judge is under the control of the referee who may instruct him as to his duties and may over rule any of his decisions. The referee may request that an unsatisfactory touch judge be replaced and he has power to order off and report to the Union a touch judge who in his opinion is guilty of misconduct.

3.  Each touch judge shall carry a flag (or other suitable object) to signal his decisions. There shall be one touch judge on each side of the ground and he shall remain in touch except when judging a kick at goal.

4.  He must hold up his flag when the ball or a player carrying it has gone into touch and must indicate the place of throw-in and which team is entitled to do so. He must also signal to the referee when the ball or a player carrying it has gone into touch-in-goal.

5.  The touch judge shall lower his flag when the ball has been thrown in except on the following occasions when he must keep it raised:
    a.  when the player throwing in the ball puts any part of either foot in the field-of-play,
    b.  when the ball has not been thrown in by the team entitled to do so,
    c.  when, at a quick throw-in, the ball that went into touch is replaced by another or is handled by anyone other than the players.
    It is for the referee to decide whether or not the ball has been thrown in from the correct place.

6. In matches in which a national representative team is playing and in such domestic matches for which a Union gives express permission, and where referees recognised by the Union are appointed as touch judges, the touch judges shall report incidents of foul play and misconduct under law 26(3) to the referee for the match.

    A touch judge shall signal such an incident to the referee by raising his flag to a horizontal position pointing directly across the field at a right angle to the touch line. The touch judge must remain in touch and continue to carry out his other functions until the next stoppage in play when the referee shall consult him regarding the incident. The referee may then take whatever action he deems appropriate and any consequent penalties shall be in accordance with Law 26(3).

7. When a kick at goal from a try or penalty kick is being taken both touch judges must assist the referee by signalling the result of the kick. One touch judge shall stand at or behind each of the goal posts and shall raise his flag if the ball goes over the crossbar.

# LAW 6
## *The art of touch judging*

### Touch judging at club level
The aim of this is to improve the three man team of the touch judges and the referee so that:

1. each member of the team contributes to specific aspects of the game,

2. decision making in the corner post situation is improved, and

3. there is a uniform and consistent approach adopted to touch judging.

## Touch judges' duties

1. There shall be two touch judges for every match.

2. There shall be one touch judge on each side of the ground and he shall remain in touch except when judging a kick at goal.

3. A touch judge must hold up his flag when the ball or a player carrying it has gone into touch. He must indicate the place of throw-in by standing opposite the place about five metres into touch. He must indicate which team is entitled to throw in the ball by pointing with his free hand in the direction of the goal line of that team.

4. The touch judge shall lower his flag when the ball has been thrown in except on the following occasions when he must keep it raised:
   a. when the player throwing in the ball puts any part of either foot in the field-of-play,
   b. when the ball has not been thrown in by the team entitled to do so, and
   c. when, at a quick throw-in, the ball that went into touch is replaced by another or is handled by anyone other than players.
   d. It is for the referee to decide whether or not the ball has been thrown in from the correct place.

5. The touch judge must also signal to the referee when the ball or a player carrying it has gone into touch-in-goal, or onto or over the dead-ball line by waving his flag in the direction of the twenty-two metres line, to signal that a drop-out should be awarded.

6. When a kick at goal from a try or penalty kick is being taken both touch judges must assist the referee by signalling the result of the kick. One touch judge shall stand at or behind each goal post and shall raise his flag if the ball goes over the crossbar.

## Positioning

*General comments*

There are two general issues which need to be addressed as they have such an impact on the role of touch judges and on how well it is performed. First, just as the referee is required to 'read' a game, so too must a touch judge in order to be in the correct position at the right time. It is essential for each touch judge to get quickly into position by anticipating in which direction play is likely to proceed. To achieve this, each touch judge must concentrate completely on what he is doing; as with refereeing, it is the ability to concentrate which is the most important factor influencing whether or not a good job is done.

Many touch judges have a tendency to 'referee' or 'watch' the game in progress, instead of concentrating on the job in hand. Often the failure of a touch judge to perform up to expectations can be put down to this lack of concentration. It is now important for touch judges, just as it is for referees, to concentrate fully for the whole game.

Secondly, remember there is a three man team operating – the two touch judges and the referee. Within this team, it is the responsibility of each touch judge to help the referee *and* the other touch judge. It is also the referee's responsibility to use his judges to the maximum extent possible!

*Kick-off*

The touch judge on the side to which the ball is expected to be kicked should stand about three to four metres in touch on the receiving team's ten metre line. If the ball goes into touch on the full he should signal this by waving his flag back towards the half-way line. If there is any doubt about whether or not the ball was touched in flight before it went into touch, he should signal that the ball is in touch, but not signal which team should throw the ball in. The referee then has the opportunity to indicate which team should throw in the ball; otherwise attacking ball in.

Also, if it is a long kick, the touch judge will need to move quickly downfield towards where the ball pitches, as he may have to make a touch decision if the defending team puts the ball into touch.

The touch judge on the other touch line should stand on the receiving team's twenty two metres line. This will allow him to cover a long kick more easily, especially if a 'dead-ball line' decision is needed. (The referee of course should use the touch judge for this purpose!). However, he has to be alert for an unexpected kick towards his touch line. His role is then as described for the near side touch judge.

*Drop-out*
The touch judge on the side to which the ball is expected to be kicked should stand three or four metres in touch in line with the receiving forwards. If the ball goes out on the full this should be indicated by waving the flag in the direction of the twenty two metre line. Also if it is a long kick, especially towards his touch line, he will need to move quickly downfield.

The touch judge on the other side should be downfield towards the half-way line as long drop-outs usually go towards that touch line.

Both touch judges must be alert for quick drop-outs.

*Line-out*
The touch judge on the side where the ball is going out indicates the line-of-touch. In addition, he must remain aware of where the line-of-touch is and be prepared to indicate the place if another line-out is called or if a scrum or penalty ensues from the line-out.

*Scrum*
The touch judges must anticipate which way the play will move and be ready to move quickly with the ensuing play. Normally, the side putting in the ball will win it, and touch judges should be able to 'read' the game to determine towards

which side the ball will be played. The positioning described under general play will then apply.

### Ruck and maul

The positioning for the ruck/maul is essentially the same as for the scrum, except that the referee is more likely to move around. Touch judges must be prepared to alter their positions to give themselves a different view from the referee.

Another significant difference is that rucks/mauls may take place close to touch. Concentrate on the player with the ball as the maul forms and the position of his feet. Make sure he still has the ball when he goes into touch. Rucks are somewhat simpler as the ball is on the ground. When in doubt signal that the ball is in touch, but do not signal which team should throw the ball in. The referee then has the opportunity to indicate which team should throw in the ball; otherwise attacking ball in.

### In general play

Normally in general play the touch judges should be positioned behind play. The touch judges on the touch line to which the play is moving should be slightly behind the play, concentrating on the back-play. Positioning in this manner results in all facets of the play being observed.

With kicks taken in general play from near the twenty-two metres line, the important decision is whether or not the kick was taken behind the twenty-two metres line. The near side touch judge should ensure he is in a position to make this judgement, even if this means he is well behind the ball as it crosses the touch line.

If there is a stoppage of play for a matter such as an injury, the touch judges should stand on the line-of-touch in order to indicate to the referee the line-of-touch on which play should restart.

*Penalty and free kick*

The touch judge on the side to which the ball is expected to be kicked should position himself far enough downfield so that, if possible, the ball is coming towards him. If there is any possibility of the kick going as far as the corner post, he should go downfield and stand in touch-in-goal near the corner post. He is then in perfect position to judge whether the ball goes into touch-in-goal (then a drop-out). If the ball crosses the line fifteen metres from the corner post, it is a simple matter to run up there knowing there had been no chance of getting egg on his face!

Generally speaking, it is better to go downfield and let kicks come towards you, but make some exception for free kicks taken by a player in his own twenty two. If the free kick is charged down, it can very quickly turn into a corner post decision.

The touch judge on the other side should move downfield some way just in case the ball is kicked unexpectedly towards that touch line.

*Kick at Goal*

A goal is scored if the ball goes over the crossbar. If the ball goes over the top of the upright, it is not a goal. If the ball is touched in flight by an opposition player and then goes over, it is still a goal. Should a ball go over the crossbar and then be blown back, it is also a goal.

Touch judges who should work in tandem, and should position themselves behind the uprights viewing the ball on the inside of the upright. They should remain stationary, if possible, as it is then easier to make 'close' decisions. As the ball comes towards your post call 'mine' and as the ball passes inside your upright and over the crossbar call 'yes'; both flags should then be raised simultaneously. Otherwise call 'no'; both touch judges should indicate this by keeping their flags at their sides.

After an unsuccessful penalty kick, the touch judges should *not* move away until the ball becomes dead or play moves away, as they may obstruct a player. They should watch the ball and if it goes over the dead-ball line, it is indicated by waving the flag in the direction of the twenty-two metres line.

### Corner post situation

Touch decisions relating to In-goal are critical. Although they may only occur once or twice during a game, they can have a vital consequence on the game's result, because in most cases the decision is a try or a twenty-two metres drop-out – a world of difference. Of course it is the referee's prerogative to make such decisions but the touch judge's action or lack thereof (see later) will provide the basis for the referee's decision. It is essential, therefore, that he attempts to be in the best position possible to judge these important situations.

In general play, the touch judge on the side to which play is moving will be attempting to be just slightly behind play. In these circumstances at the corner post situation the touch judge should take up a stationary position about five metres in touch and about five metres on the field-of-play side of the goal line. From this ideal stationary position he is able to concentrate fully on what is happening without the prospect of becoming entangled with the cover defence.

However, from set play reasonably close to the goal line the touch judge may be able to take up a position in touch-in-goal about five metres from the touch-in-goal line and about two metres on the In-goal side of the goal line. From this position the timing of the grounding of the ball in relation to hitting the corner post is clear because the ball should be in view. Also, from this position the touch judge is normally in the referee's scope of vision. There is little doubt that this 'in front' position offers the best view for the touch judge, but it is difficult to reach this position in most instances.

The responsibility of the touch judge near the corner post is:
1. to judge whether a player carrying the ball goes into touch before the corner post, which is signalled by raising the flag immediately.
2. to judge whether a player carrying the ball hits the corner post before or after grounding the ball in the In-goal area – if the post is hit before the ball is grounded, this is signalled by waving the flag in the direction of the twenty-two metres line.
3. to judge if the ball went into touch-in-goal which is signalled by waving the flag in the direction of the twenty-two metres line.

Attention should be riveted on the ball carrier, with particular reference to the ball and his feet. The object is to observe the timing of the action of grounding the ball in relation to striking the corner post, and to observe whether the player stepped into touch (ie on or beyond the touch line) before grounding the ball or being tackled into the corner post.

It is the timing of grounding the ball in relation to striking the corner post that is critical and a few hints may help.
1. If the player dives over the goal line with the ball in his possession and his legs hit the corner post as a result of an attempted tackle, there is a high probability of a try as the ball carrier will be sloping downwards with the ball held lower than the line of his body. In general then, in a dive over situation, the further away from the ball the player's body makes contact with the corner post the more likely a try.
2. When in doubt, not out (ie any 50/50 decisions tend to go with the attacking side and a try is given).
3. If the corner post leans into the field of play and a ball carrier strikes it but would not have if it had been standing upright at 90 degrees, this is simply bad luck.
4. As noted in the law the flag is not part of the corner post.

5. The direction of the tackler may be a useful guide. If side on, it is likely to be a tight decision especially if the tackler grabs the ball carrier anywhere near the ball. If the tackle comes from behind it may simply give more impetus to the player attempting to ground the ball.

6. If there is no corner post (eg fallen down), do not imagine one – as long as the ball is grounded fairly, it is a try or touchdown.

7. If a player dives over a goal line to apply downward pressure to a loose ball, there is no problem if he hits the corner post in doing so, providing he does not pick the ball up – remember a try can be scored from touch, or touch-in-goal, if a player exerts downward pressure on a loose ball lying In-goal.

Although it is the referee's responsibility, touch judges can give valuable assistance to the referee by indicating their opinion of whether or not a try has been fairly scored. If in the touch judge's opinion a try is not scored the touch judge should indicate his opinion to the referee by standing near to the touch line some three to five metres back from the corner post moving towards the twenty-two metres line. If the touch judge is of the opinion a fair try had been scored he should indicate this to the referee by standing in touch-in-goal past the corner post moving towards the dead-ball line.

**Other matters**
The following points are separate matters which are not covered elsewhere.

1. Carry a whistle.

2. Keep the ball boys off the touch line – five metres back is a good distance. Don't let ball boys interfere with quick throw-ins. However, it's not your responsibility to decide who should or should not be the ball boys.

3. On open fields, don't let spectators encroach on the playing area.

4. Ensure you keep the time, in case of:
   — reference by referee
   — need to replace the referee.

**Conclusion**

Remember, Club touch judges have two main jobs:
   — to adjudicate on touch
   — to assist the referee and the other touch judge

In order to do these jobs properly, no longer should touch judges think and position themselves as do referees. Position yourself to provide the *team work* necessary to help the referee and your fellow touch judge.

# LAW 7
## *Mode of Play*

A match is started by a kick-off, after which any player who is on-side may at any time:

— catch or pick up the ball and run with it,

— pass, throw or knock the ball to another player,

— kick or otherwise propel the ball,

— tackle, push or shoulder an opponent holding the ball,

— fall on the ball,

— take part in scrummage, ruck, maul or line-out provided he does so in accordance with these Laws.

## LAW 7

Law 7 is the law which very simply lays down the method of playing the game. It does not attempt to explain law but simply states what any player who is in an on-side position can legitimately attempt.

The one note that the law does make is that if a player hands the ball to a team member, without any propulsion or throwing of the ball, then it does not constitute a pass. In other words, if the ball carrier *hands* the ball to a team mate, without any propulsion, it is not a pass even if the player receiving the ball is in front of the original ball carrier. For a pass to be a pass the ball must be propelled through the air from one player to another. Handing the ball to another player does not constitute a pass although the referee must be aware of any accidental off-side situation .

# LAW 8
## *Advantage*

The referee shall not whistle for an infringement during play which is followed by an advantage gained by the non-offending team. An advantage must be either territorial or such possession of the ball as constitutes an obvious tactical advantage. A mere opportunity to gain advantage is not sufficient.

# LAW 8

It would appear that the shortest law in the book should be one of the easiest to apply but in practice nothing could be further from the truth. The referee is given a wide discretion as to what constitutes an advantage and what does not. Advantage is not limited to territorial position nor indeed to possession of the ball but to a combination of both. The notes to the law state that the referee is the sole judge of whether or not an advantage has been gained. To apply the law correctly, a referee must have a good understanding and feel for the game. He must try and identify whether an advantage which he allowed for one team is in fact an advantage to the other team.

By its very nature, the advantage law is subjective and not as clear cut as most of the other laws. What is seen as advantage through one team's eyes is not necessarily visualised by the other team as an advantage. Interpretation of the advantage law varies from country to country and in fact from referee to referee. The whole theory behind the advantage law is to keep the game moving, keep the ball alive and by so doing allow the non-offending team the possible chance of benefitting from a mistake or infringement by their opponents.

Advantage can be played from nearly every aspect of the game of rugby. There are very few exceptions where advantage cannot be played. The following are laid down in law as occasions when advantage does not apply:

1. When the ball or a player carrying the ball touches the referee and the referee considers either team has gained an unfair advantage. There could be occasions where the ball or the player carrying it does in fact touch the referee and play is allowed to continue. This could only happen if the referee decided that no unfair advantage accrued to either side.

2. When the ball emerges from either end of the tunnel at a scrummage without having been played. The scrummage law dictates that if the ball is put into the scrummage and comes out at either end of the tunnel it shall be put in again unless a free kick or penalty has been awarded.

3. When a player is accidentally off-side. A player is accidentally off-side if, while being in an off-side position, he cannot avoid, because of the speed of the game, being touched by the ball or by one of his own players carrying the ball. Again (as in exception 1), play should be allowed to continue unless the infringing team obtains an unfair advantage. This law was altered a few years back and we now have the situation prevailing that it is no longer obligatory for the referee to award a scrummage for accidentally off-side every time the ball carrier runs into one of his own players who is in an off-side position.

4. When a scrummage collapses and the ball is still within the confines of the scrummage. Although not specifically stated in law, if the scrummage collapses, the referee is obliged to blow his whistle immediately. By this action the law makers have implied that advantage cannot be played from a collapsed scrum.

These then, according to law, are the very few occasions when the referee may not apply advantage. In every other situation, depending on certain circumstances, for example foul play or serious injury, the referee can apply the advantage law. The referee should not blow his whistle immediately just because he sees an infringement, rather he should allow play to continue to see if the non-offending team gain an advantage. If no advantage occurs, the referee should always bring the game back for the original infringement.

Although the advantage law is the envy of many other sporting organisations, it is sometimes difficult to play advantage particularly if either the referee or the players are not mentally attuned to the possibility of advantage. A referee can help to overcome this by trying to transmit to the players, through his attitude, actions and speech, his keenness to allow advantage in every possibly situation, while players should always continue to play until they hear the referee blow his whistle.

Now let us look at the advantage law as far as its philosophy is concerned and in particular with the very few occasions when advantage cannot be played according to the law book.

As explained previously, because the application of the advantage law is left solely to the referee, there will be differences in interpretation especially from country to country, therefore the most important thing that a referee must be is consistent throughout a game however he applies the advantage law.

Certain aspects in applying advantage are clear cut. For example, if side A knock the ball on and side B immediately gather the ball and kick it forty or fifty metres down the park and into touch, it is obvious that the referee would allow the advantage and award the touch. What happens however, if side B gather the ball and only manage to find touch ten metres down the park? Would the referee award the touch with side A throwing the ball in or would he award the scrummage with side B putting the ball in? In most cases the latter alternative would be the option although the referee would have to take into consideration whether side B were being out-scrummaged or whether they had been winning all the line-out ball up to that time.

Lets take another situation when side A knock on, again side B gather the ball but this time they decide to pass the ball along the three-quarter line where it is knocked on by their winger without the ball having crossed the gain line. In such a situation, the referee should bring play back and award the scrummage for the initial knock-on by side A. Advantage, according the law book, ' . . . must be either territorial or such advantage as constitutes an obvious tactical advantage'. In this instance the non-offending team ie side B, has neither gained a territorial nor a tactical advantage. Similarly, in a situation where a hooker lifts his foot early while striking for the ball but loses the scrum to the other side whose scrum half then knocks the ball on while picking it up at his number eight's feet, the referee should penalise the initial infringement of the foot up because no territorial or tactical advantage has been gained by the non-offending team.

Let us look at another example. The attacking team is in the process of winning a ruck inside their opponent's twenty-two metres line in front of the posts. The defending scrum half is caught off-side, but does not prevent the attacking scrum half from getting the ball and passing it away. The ball is quickly passed out to the attacking side's winger who is pushed into touch short of the try line. In this situation, although territorial advantage has been gained, the real advantage should be tactical and therefore a penalty kick (and a certain three points) should be awarded back at the place of infringement. The only advantage from a certain three-point penalty kick in this situation would be a four-point and possibly with a conversion, a six-point try. Therefore advantage should be allowed to run for a reasonable time to see if true advantage takes place. Although no time limit is laid down in law for the length of time that the referee should allow advantage to run, he must not allow play to continue for too long a period so that he has an inordinate amount of explaining to do regarding the initial infringement which the players will have forgotten about.

A similar situation to this last one would occur if instead of the non-offending side running the ball, their outside half attempted a dropped goal which missed. Again the referee should bring play back and award the penalty for the initial infringement because the non-offending team has not profited from the actions of the offending side.

Certain countries would argue that in allowing the non-offending team to have possession of the ball is a tactical advantage and therefore if they, due to their inability, do not profit from this situation and the referee brings the play back to award the original infringement, the non-offending team is having 'two bites at the cherry'. But remember, the law states that ' . . . a mere opportunity to gain advantage is not sufficient'.

In coming to a decision about advantage, the referee must take many things into account, either consciously or subconsciously. Among the variables that will enter the equation will be:

1. Time in the game.
2. Relative strengths of the teams.
3. Position of play on the field, for example proximity to goal lines.
4. State of the game, for example score and length of time to be played.
5. Nature of the offence, for example foul play or technical infringement.

It is interesting to note that, historically, it was the captain of the non-offending team who decided whether or not he wanted the game to continue after an infringement. The referee therefore, in deciding whether or not advantage should be played from a specific situation, should put himself in the position of the non-offending team and ask himself, 'If I were the non-offending team would I want play to continue?'

# LAW 9
## *Ball or Player Touching Referee*

1. If the ball or a player carrying it touches the referee in the field-of-play, play shall continue unless the referee considers either team has gained an advantage in which case he shall order a scrummage. The team which last played the ball shall put it in.

2. a. If the ball in a player's possession or a player carrying it touches the referee in that player's In-goal, a touch-down shall be awarded.
   b. If a player carrying the ball in his opponents' In-goal touches the referee before grounding the ball, a try shall be awarded at that place.

## LAW 9

This particular law is divided into two distinct parts. Firstly, the ball or the player carrying the ball touching the referee in the field-of-play and secondly, if the same happens in either of the In-goal areas.

Just because the ball or a player carrying the ball comes in contact with the referee in the field-of-play does not necessitate the refee blowing for an infringement. Unless the referee deems that either side gain an unfair advantage from the situation, play should be allowed to continue. If for example the ball carrier comes in contact with the referee and there is no member of the opposition close to the incident, play should be allowed to continue. Similarly, if there is an opposition player who would have been close enough to tackle the ball carrier but was prevented from doing so because the referee was in the way after being touched by the ball carrier, the referee should award a scrummage.

If a loose ball strikes the referee and is then played by either team, the referee has to decide whether in the act of the ball touching him, either of the sides then took possession of the ball to the detriment of the other. Again, if it was deemed one side gained an advantage, a scrummage should be awarded. In all cases the team who last played the ball, either by passing, kicking or carrying it should put the ball into the resultant scrummage.

The second part of the law deals with the situation if the ball or ball carrier touch the referee in either of the In-goal areas. If this happens a touch-down should be awarded. If an attacking player with the ball in his possession touches the referee, a try should be awarded at the place the contact was made. If the player carrying the ball is a defender, a touch-down should be awarded thereafter, depending on circumstances, a scrum-five or drop-out would be the decision. Likewise, if the ball is in In-goal but not held by a player and touches the referee, either a try or touch-down would be awarded depending, in the referee's judgement, on who would have got to the ball first. The referee should, in coming to his decision, be aware that the law requires him to ensure that a touch-down, either for the attackers or the defenders would have been secured if the ball had not touched the referee. If the ball was going to go over the dead-ball line or into touch-in-goal, before being grounded by a player, and was prevented from doing so by the referee, no touch-down or try should be awarded.

Although we have so far only referred to the ball or player carrying the ball touching the referee, the same criteria apply if the ball or ball carrier come into contact with a touch judge or spectator in the In-goal area. Although no reference is made to such an incident happening in the field-of-play, common sense suggests that the correct award here would be a scrummage, with the side who last played the ball having the put in.

If the ball touches a spectator in In-goal and the referee is in doubt as to whether to award a try or a touch-down, he should assume the spectator is a home spectator and the award should be made in favour of the visiting team whether they are defending or attacking.

# LAW 10
## *Kick-Off*

Kick-off is (a) a place kick taken from the centre of the half-way line by the team which has the right to start the match or by the opposing team on the resumption of play after the half-time interval or by the defending team after a goal has been scored, or (b) a drop kick taken at or from behind the centre of the half-way line by the defending team after an unconverted try.

1. The ball must be kicked from the correct place and by the correct form of kick; otherwise it shall be kicked off again.

2. The ball must reach the opponents' ten metres line, unless first played by an opponent; otherwise it shall be kicked off again, or a scrummage formed at the centre, at the opponents' option. If it reaches the ten metres line and is then blown back, play shall continue.

3. If the ball pitches directly into touch, touch-in-goal or over or on the dead-ball line, the opposing team may accept the kick, have the ball kicked off again, or have a scrummage formed at the centre.

4. The *kicker's team* must be behind the ball when kicked; otherwise a scrummage shall be formed at the centre.

5. The *opposing team* must stand on or behind the ten metres line. If they are in front of that line or if they charge before the ball has been kicked, it shall be kicked off again.

## LAW 10

This particular law deals with the kick-off after a try has been scored and the requirements that must take place so that the ball can be brought back into play.

The first statement concerns the type of kicks to be taken, either a place kick for a converted try or else a drop kick for an unconverted try. There is no choice. Players who are better at place kicking rather than drop kicking and vice versa cannot opt for a preference and should not be allowed to by the referee.

The law states that the ball must be kicked by the correct form of kick and at the correct place. Referees should be strict in ensuring that the ball is kicked from the centre of the half-way line. In allowing players to deviate from the mark he allows an unfair advantage for the side who are kicking off.

As far as the player who is taking the kick is concerned, a good referee will tell such a player if he is taking the wrong type of kick or if he is taking the kick from the wrong place rather than waiting for the kick to be taken. If either of these two points are infringed, the referee should order the ball to be kicked off again.

From either a place kick or a drop kick, the ball must reach the opponents' ten metres line otherwise the opposition have the option of a scrummage on the centre, with their put in, or else the kick to be retaken. If the ball does not reach the ten metres line and is first played by a member of the non-kicking off side, they take all the consequences and they have relinquished their choice of retaken kick or scrummage. If, for example, the non-kicking off side play the ball prior to its reaching the ten metres line and then immediately knock it on, the correct decision would be a scrummage for the knock on, not the option for the ball not travelling the required ten metres.

In part three of the law, it is a requirement that, from the kick-off, the ball must not pitch directly into touch, touch-in-goal or over the dead-ball area without first bouncing or touching a player. If the ball pitches directly into one of these three locations, then the opposition have three options. They can have the original kick retaken, they can choose a scrummage at the centre of the half-way line with their put-in or they can accept the kick. If they accept the kick, we must be aware of the position in the field where the ball can be brought back into play. If the ball pitches into touch, the option is a line-out on the half-way line with the non-offending team throwing the ball in. If, on the other hand, the ball pitches directly into touch-in-goal or over the dead-ball line, the correct decision is a drop-out on the twenty two metres line. Referees should ensure when ascertaining which option the non-offending team wish, that it is the captain and the captain alone who decides which one of the options his team wishes. Before the captain expresses his choice, referees, players and touch judges should always be aware that the obvious choice is not necessarily the one which will be made.

In part four of the law, the position that the kicker's team take up prior to the kick-off is indicated. The kicker's team must be behind the ball before it is kicked otherwise a scrummage shall be formed at the centre of the half-way line with the non-offending side putting the ball in. Note that in this instance, the non-offending team do not have the option of the kick being retaken. As with the other aspects of law, a good referee should await to see if any advantage accrues.

# LAW 11
## *Method of Scoring*

**Try**

A try is scored by first grounding the ball in the opponents' In-goal.

A try shall be awarded if one would probably have been scored but for foul play by the opposing team.

**Goal**

A goal is scored by kicking the ball over the opponents' crossbar and between the goal posts from the field-of-play by any place kick or drop kick, except a kick-off, drop-out or free kick, without touching the ground or any player of the kicker's team.

A goal is scored if the ball has crossed the bar notwithstanding a prior offence of the opposing team.

A goal is scored if the ball has crossed the bar, even though it may have been blown backwards afterwards, and whether it has touched the crossbar or either goal post or not.

A goal may be awarded if the ball is illegally touched by any player of the opposing team and if the referee considers that a goal would otherwise probably have been scored.

*The scoring values are as follows:*

| | |
|---|---|
| A try | 4 points |
| A goal scored after a try | 2 points |
| A goal from a penalty kick | 3 points |
| A dropped goal otherwise obtained | 3 points |

## LAW 11

This law defines the two methods of scoring, which occur in the game, together with the value of such scores.

A *try* is stated as being scored by a player first grounding the ball in the opponents' In-goal. The definition of grounding the ball is given in Law 12. The law also states that the referee *shall* award a try if one would probably have been scored but for foul play. This form of scoring is termed a penalty try and is defined later in Law 12. The areas of foul play for which the referee shall award a penalty try are contained in Law 26. It should be noted that the word *shall* is used in the law indicating that the referee has no option but to award a try if one would probably have been scored but for foul play.

The scoring value of a try, including a penalty try, is four points.

A *goal* can be either a penalty goal, a dropped goal or a conversion after a try or penalty try. A goal cannot be scored from a kick-off, drop-out or directly from a free kick. The scoring values for the different types of kick are defined within the law as being three points for a goal from a penalty kick or a dropped goal and two points for a conversion after a try or penalty try.

If, say because of a strong wind, an attempted goal kick crosses the bar and is blown back over the bar the kick is good, so long as the whole of the ball has crossed the plane of the bar.

If, after a goal kick is attempted, the opposition touch the ball but do not prevent the ball from going over the bar, then the referee shall still award the goal. If, on the other hand, the ball touches the ground and bounces over the bar or if the ball touches a team member of the player attempting the goal kick and goes over the bar, then the goal shall be disallowed.

As with other laws, if the referee deems that the ball is illegally prevented from crossing the bar by a player of the opposing team, then he has the power under Law 12 to award the goal.

# LAW 12
## *Try and Touch-Down*

Grounding the ball is the act of a player who
a. while holding the ball in his hand (or hands) or arm (or arms) brings the ball in contact with the ground, or
b. while the ball is on the ground either:
— places his hand (or hands) or arm (or arms) on it with downward pressure, or
— falls upon it and the ball is anywhere under the front of his body from waist to neck inclusive.

Picking up the ball from the ground is not grounding it.

A. TRY
1. A player who is on-side scores a try when:
— he carries the ball into his opponents' In-goal, or
— the ball is in his opponents' In-goal, and he first grounds it there.

2. The scoring of a try includes the following cases:
a. if a player carries, passes, knocks or kicks the ball into his In-goal and an opponent first grounds it,
b. if, at a scrummage or ruck, a team is pushed over its goal line and before the ball has emerged it is first grounded in In-goal by an attacking player,
c. if the momentum of a player, when tackled, carries him into his opponents' In-goal and he grounds the ball there first,
d. if a player first grounds the ball on his opponents' goal line or if the ball is in contact with the ground and a goal post,
e. if a tackle occurs in such a position that the tackled player whilst complying with the Law is able to place the ball on or over the goal line.

3. If a player grounds the ball in his opponents' In-goal and picks it up again, a try is scored where it was first grounded.

4. A try may be scored by a player who is in touch or in touch-in-goal provided he is not carrying the ball.

B.   **PENALTY TRY**
A penalty try shall be awarded between the posts if but for foul
play by the defending team:
—  a try would probably have been scored, or
—  it would probably have been scored in a more
    favourable position than that where the ball was
    grounded.

C.   **TOUCH-DOWN**
1.  A touch-down occurs when a player first grounds the ball in his
In-goal.

2   After a touch-down, play shall be restarted either by a drop-out
or a scrummage, as provided in Law 14.

D.   **SCRUMMAGE AFTER GROUNDING IN CASE OF DOUBT**
Where there is doubt as to which team first grounded the ball in In-
goal, a scrummage shall be formed five metres from the goal line
opposite the place where the ball was grounded. The attacking team
shall put in the ball.

# LAW 12

This law covers the act of scoring a try, by an attacking player,
or securing a touch-down if a defensive player. The first
section of the law defines exactly what is meant by the proper
grounding of the ball in order to obtain a touch-down.

Firstly a player who has the ball in his posession either in his
hands or in his arms brings the ball into contact with the
ground. The old phrasing of exerting downward pressure on
the ball is no longer applicable in this particular case, the simple
act of the player touching the ball on the ground is sufficient.

Secondly, if the ball is lying loose on the ground in the In-goal
area a player can either touch the ball down with his
hand/hands or with his arm/arms or else he can fall on the ball.
In the case of falling on the ball, the ball must be under the

front of the player's body from the area stretching from the neck to the waist. The ball being under a player's legs would not constitute a touch-down. If the ball is lying loose in In-goal the player attempting to secure a touch-down must, in this instance, exert downward pressure on the ball. Simply picking the ball up does not constitute grounding the ball.

The law is subsequently divided into three sections, firstly awarding of the try, secondly a penalty try and lastly a touch-down.

## TRY

The first obvious statement is that before a try can be scored the player who scores it must be on-side. There are no cases in this or in any of the other sections of this law where a try or touch-down can be awarded if the player attempting to secure the touch-down or try is off-side.

Tries can be scored in a variety of ways so long as the ball is properly grounded. If a defending player plays the ball into his own In-goal area he suffers all the consequences, one of which might be a try. If the ball is loose in In-goal, referees should be aware of the possibility of obstruction by a defending player in an attempt to prevent an opponent from securing a try.

If the attacking team have the ball in their possession in a scrum or ruck and they push the defending players over their own goal line a try can be awarded if they touch the ball down first. In this case it should be noted that the moment the ball touches the goal line any scrum or ruck ceases to exist and a player from either team can dive into the scrum or ruck (see Laws 20 and 21 regarding the ending of scrums and rucks). Referees must ensure that players from either team do not attempt to secure the ball in this situation until the ball has touched or crossed the line.

If a player is tackled short of the goal line but his momentum carries him into the In-goal where he grounds the ball a try can be awarded. In this instance referees must ensure that it is the player's momentum that takes him into the In-goal area and not some illegal double movement. Excess body movement either with legs or arms must be watched for by the referee. In most momentum tries, ground conditions usually play a part, therefore it is more likely to get such tries if the ground is wet and greasy rather than when the ground is hard.

A try can also be scored if the ball is placed on the goal line or is in contact with the ground and the goal post. On the line is deemed to be In-goal and therefore if an attacking player is so held that he can only place the ball on the goal line that is good enough for the referee to award a try. Similarly, if he is held in front of the goal post and places the ball on the ground so that it comes into contact with the bottom of the post, that also is deemed to be In-goal and a try can be awarded. It should be noted that it is not a try if the ball carrier is held and places the ball against the post. The ball must be in contact with the bottom of the post and the ground. There is no reference in law to the actual thickness of the padding around the post therefore any thickness is acceptable.

If a player is tackled short of the goal line he can stretch over the goal line in an attempt to ground the ball and be awarded a try. Greater reference is made to this situation in Law 18, but suffice to say that in order to obtain a try in this manner, a player must comply with the relevant part of Law 18 and his actions must be immediate.

A try can only be scored in the position the ball was first grounded. If an attacking player grounds a ball and subsequently picks it up and regrounds it in a more advantageous position, the try is awarded where the ball was first grounded. Referees should be aware of players going to ground with the ball cradled in their arms but not touching the ball down, standing up and then placing the ball in a better position. Referees should never award a try unless they actually see the ball grounded.

If the ball is loose In-goal, an attacking player can still be awarded a try even though he himself is in touch, touch-in-goal or over the dead-ball line. In these cases the player is not allowed to carry the ball prior to his touching it down.

## PENALTY TRY

If in the view of the referee, an attacking side has been prevented from scoring a try by the illegal actions of the defending team, he shall award a penalty try. The wording of the law gives the referee no option but to award a penalty try. A few seasons ago the wording was that 'the referee may award a penalty try' but the law states the referee *shall* award a penalty try. The areas of illegal play from which penalty tries might be awarded are contained in Law 26 concerning foul play. Examples could be defending players diving into a scrum before the ball has crossed the goal line, defending players collapsing a scrum when the attacking side are going for a push over try, obstruction of an attacking player etc.

If the referee awards a penalty try, the try shall be awarded as if it were scored between the posts. It should be noted that the award of the try is the penalty and not the conversion afterwards. The conversion after a penalty try award is a normal conversion kick at goal at which the defending players can charge.

## TOUCH-DOWN

For a touch-down to be awarded to a defending team, the correct grounding of the ball must be complied with. The defending player can be awarded a touch-down if either a defender or an attacker takes the ball into the defender's In-goal. If the ball is correctly grounded the referee will award either a scrum-five or a drop-out depending on the circumstances of how the ball was taken into In-goal. Reference should be made to Law 14 regarding the correct interpretation.

If the referee is in doubt as to which side touched the ball down in In-goal, he should award a scrummage on the five metres line opposite the place of doubt with the attacking side putting the ball in. Unless the referee actually sees the ball grounded immediately, he is not in a position to award a try or a touch-down and should not do so. It is unacceptable for a referee to guess what happened even although it might appear obvious, neither should a referee wait until a pile of bodies extricate themselves before he comes to a decision.

## LAW 13
### *Kick at Goal After a Try*

1.  After a try has been scored, the scoring team has the right to take a place kick or drop kick at goal, on a line through the place where the try was scored.

    If the scoring team does not take the kick, play shall be restarted by a drop kick from the centre, unless time has expired.

2.  If a kick is taken:
    a.  it must be taken without undue delay
    b.  any player including the kicker may place the ball
    c.  the *kicker's team*, except a placer, must be behind the ball when kicked
    d.  if the kicker kicks the ball from a placer's hands without the ball being on the ground, the kick is void
    e.  the *opposing team* must be behind the goal line until the kicker begins his run or offers to kick when they may charge or jump with a view to preventing a goal.

3.  Neither the kicker nor a placer shall wilfully do anything which may lead the opposing team to charge prematurely. If either does so, the charge shall not be disallowed.

## LAW 13

The first thing to state is that it is not a necessity for a kick at goal, (commonly known as a conversion kick) to be taken after a try has been scored. It is at the option of the team scoring a try whether or not they wish to attempt a kick for the extra two points. It is unusual for this to happen in a fifteen-a-side match, but it is common place in a seven-a-side match where time is of the essence and possibly another try is required to obtain a win. If a kick is declined, play shall be restarted from the half-way line with a drop kick.

The kicker is meant to kick without any undue delay. Undue delay is stated in the notes to the law as being within one minute of an indication by the kicker that he wishes to kick for goal. An indication to kick might be the kicker making a mark for the ball with his boot or if he wishes to use saw dust, sand or a tee, which he is entitled to do, the moment he requests such assistance from the side line. Referees should always ensure that kickers are not unreasonably slow in taking a kick at goal. If a player is persistently slow, he should be warned by the referee for time wasting and the kick disallowed. In any case, if the kicker takes any more than forty seconds to take the kick, any additional time should be added onto the end of that particular half as required under Law 5.

For a kick at goal after a try, the kicker's team must be behind the ball before the kick is taken. If they are not then any successful kick should be disallowed. The exception to this is in the case of a player who might be holding the ball for the kicker. This placer, so long as he is holding the ball in place, can be in front of the ball.

All the members of the opposing team must be behind their goal line prior to the kicker beginning his run up. Referees should ensure that all the opposing players are behind the line, especially in seven-a-side matches where players tend to wait on the half-way line until the kick is taken. If, on the other hand, the kicker wishes to take a quick kick at goal, possibly because of time, then he accepts all the consequences if he misses the kick. In the normal course of events, the kicker should wait until all the opposition are behind their own goal line. Once the players are so positioned, they are then allowed to charge when the kicker begins his run up in an attempt to prevent the kick succeeding. They can only charge once the kicker offers to kick, for example when the kicker begins to move forward. Referees should ensure that the players do not creep up or charge too early. If the kick is missed and the players have charged too early, then the referee should allow the kick to be retaken, this time, without the players being allowed to charge. He should also allow the kicker all the original preliminaries, for example one minute within which the kick should be taken. The player can also be allowed to change the type of kick ie from place kick to drop kick or vice versa. If the kick is successful, it should be allowed to stand.

When players are charging the kick, they are not allowed to shout in an attempt to distract the kicker. If they do and the kick is missed, another kick shall be awarded.

The kick must be taken with the ball which was in play when the try was scored unless the referee deems that that particular ball has become defective.

If the ball rolls over once the kicker has started his run, he has various options. He can either forget about the kick, he can kick the ball as it is lying on the ground no matter where it is lying or else he can pick the ball up and attempt a drop goal. If the player attempts a drop goal in this situation, referees must ensure that the kicker kicks the ball on the line through the place where the try was scored. None of the above options are available if the ball rolls over and rolls into touch. If this happens, the kick at goal should be disallowed.

For the kick at goal to be successful, the whole of the ball must pass between the posts and over the bar, even if it is then blown back. A kick is successful even if the ball is touched by the defending team prior to it crossing the bar.

# LAW 14
## *In-Goal*

In-goal is the area bounded by a goal line, touch-in-goal lines and dead-ball line. It includes the goal line and goal posts but excludes touch-in-goal lines and dead-ball line.

Touch-in-goal occurs when the ball or a player carrying it touches a corner post or a touch-in-goal line or the ground or a person or object on or beyond it. The flag is not part of the corner post.

### Five metres scrummage

1.  If a player carrying the ball in In-goal is so held that he cannot ground the ball, a scrummage shall be formed five metres from the goal line opposite the place where he was held. The attacking team shall put in the ball.

2.  a. If a defending player heels, kicks, carries, passes or knocks the ball over his goal line and it there becomes dead except where:
    — a try is scored, or
    — he wilfully knocks or throws the ball from the field-of-play into touch-in-goal or over his dead-ball line, or

    b. if a defending player in In-goal has his kick charged down by an attacking player after:
    — he carried the ball back from the field-of-play, or
    — a defending player put it into In-goal and the ball is then touched down or goes into touch-in-goal or over the dead-ball line, or

    c. if a defending player carrying the ball in the field-of-play is forced into his In-goal and he then touches down, or

    d. if, at a scrummage or ruck, a defending team with the ball in its possession is pushed over its goal line and before the ball has emerged first grounds it in In-goal, a scrummage shall be formed five metres from the goal line opposite the place where the ball or a player carrying it crossed the goal line. The attacking team shall put in the ball.

## Drop-out

3. Except where the ball is knocked on or thrown forward in the field of play or In-goal, if an attacking player kicks, carries or passes the ball and it travels into his opponents In-goal either directly or having touched a defender who does not wilfully attempt to stop, catch or kick it, and it is there

   — grounded by a defending player, or

   — goes into touch-in-goal or over the dead-ball line

   a. drop-out shall be awarded.

## Penalties

a. A penalty try shall be awarded when by foul play in In-goal the defending team has prevented a try which otherwise would *probably* have been scored.

b. A try shall be disallowed and a penalty kick awarded, if a try would *probably not* have been gained but for foul play by the attacking team.

c. For foul play in In-goal while the ball is out of play the penalty kick shall be awarded at the place where play would otherwise have restarted and, in addition, the player shall either be ordered off or cautioned that he will be sent off if he repeats the offence.

d. For wilfully charging or obstructing in In-goal a player who has just kicked the ball the penalty shall be:

   — a penalty kick in the field-of-play five metres from the goal line opposite the place of infringement, or, at the option of the non-offending team,

   — a penalty kick where the ball alights as provided under Law 26(3) Penalty (ii)(b).

e. For other infringements in In-goal, the penalty shall be the same as for a similar infringement in the field-of-play except that the mark for a penalty kick or free kick shall be in the field-of-play five metres from the goal line opposite the place of infringement and the place of any scrummage shall be five metres from the goal line opposite the place of infringement but not within five metres of the touch line.

# LAW 14

The In-goal area as defined in Law 14 is that rectangular area bounded by the goal line, the touch-in-goal lines and the dead-ball line. It includes the goal-line but does not include the touch-in-goal lines nor the dead-ball line.

In other words, if an attacking player with the ball grounds it on the goal line a try can be awarded. It has to be pointed out that a try can also be awarded in this situation if the attacking player grounds the ball and it is in contact with the goal post and the ground. The bottom of the post, including any protective padding around it, is classified as being part of the goal line. The thickness of the padding is irrelevant.

The touch-in-goal lines and the dead-ball line are not part of the In-goal area, so if the ball or a player carrying the ball touches either of these lines, the ground or a person or object beyond these lines or indeed the corner posts, the ball is either in touch-in-goal or dead.

So let us now look at certain aspects of the law in detail.

If any player, of either team, carrying the ball in In-goal is so held that he cannot ground the ball the referee should award a scrummage. The scrummage shall be awarded five metres from the goal line opposite the place where the player was held. The attacking team shall put the ball into the scrummage. A similar award is made if the referee cannot see the ball or if he is in doubt as to which team, either attacking or defending first grounded the ball in In-goal.

If a defending player plays the ball into his own In-goal and the ball becomes dead either by it being touched down or by going into touch-in-goal or over the dead-ball line, a scrummage shall be awarded to the attacking side five metres from the goal line, but in this instance the scrummage shall be awarded where the ball or the player carrying the ball first crossed the goal line. The situation could arise where a defending team play the ball into In-goal and then proceed to pass the ball along their three-quarter line and then grounding it while still In-goal some distance from where the ball went into In-goal originally. The referee will award the scrummage back where the ball originally crossed the line and not opposite the point where the ball was eventually grounded. It should be noted that if a defending player carries the ball into his own In-goal and his kick to touch is charged down by an attacking player, who is either in In-goal *or* in the field-of-play, and the ball goes dead a scrummage to the attacking side should be awarded opposite the place the ball crossed the line originally. The attacking player's position is irrelevant. If a defending player wilfully puts the ball back into his own In-goal, he accepts all the consequences of taking that action.

If when the ball is In-goal, a defending player wilfully knocks or throws the ball into touch-in-goal or over the dead-ball line he shall be penalised either by the award of a penalty try, if the referee deems that the defending player's actions prevented a try which otherwise would *probably* have been scored or by the award of a penalty kick to the attacking side five metres from the goal line opposite the place of infringement but not within five metres of the touch line.

If an attacking player kicks, carries or passes the ball and it travels into his opponents In-goal where it is then grounded by a defending player or it goes into touch-in-goal or over the dead-ball line a drop-out shall be awarded. The award shall be the same even if the ball on its way to In-goal touches a defender who does not wilfully attempt to stop it, catch it or kick it.

If an attacking player knocks the ball on in In-goal and the ball is then made dead by a player of either team, the referee shall award a scrummage five metres from the goal line opposite the place where the knock-on occurred. The *defending* team shall put the ball in. This part of the law was changed recently.

Previously a drop-out would have been the award, but this has now been altered. An example of this would be if an attacker and defender were running for a loose ball, both players dive for the ball, which is In-goal, and the ball hits the attacking player's hand and goes forward. A five metre scrum with the defending side putting the ball in would be the correct decision given by the referee.

Many people wonder whether or not a mark can be awarded In-goal. The answer is yes, but certain guide lines have to be adhered to. Firstly, if the resultant free kick is made dead before it has crossed the goal line, the attacking side shall be awarded a scrummage five metres from the goal line opposite where it was made dead. The ball can be made dead by a defending player touching it down after it has been kicked or if the ball goes into touch-in-goal or over the dead-ball line. Secondly, the attacking side are allowed to stand five metres from the goal line with a view to preventing the kick from being taken. This could mean that if a mark is made, say two metres into In-goal, the attacking side would only be seven metres away from the mark and similarly, if the mark was made ten metres into In-goal, the attacking side would be fifteen metres from the mark. This was a ruling made recently by the International Board.

The intentions of the alterations to the In-goal law was to prevent the In-goal area being looked upon as being different to the field-of-play. Therefore players can be off-side in In-goal and forward passes and knocks-on will be dealt with as if they occurred in the field-of-play. For most infringements In-goal, the penalty shall be the same as for a similar infringement in the field-of-play except that the mark for a penalty kick, free kick or scrummage shall be in the field-of-play five metres from the goal line opposite the place of infringement. The mark for a penalty kick cannot be given In-goal.

# LAW 15
## *Drop-Out*

**A drop-out is a drop kick awarded to the defending team.**

1. The drop kick must be taken from anywhere on or behind the twenty two metres line; otherwise the ball shall be dropped out again.

2. The ball must cross the twenty two metres line; otherwise the opposing team may have it dropped out again, or have a scrummage formed at the centre of the twenty two metres line. If it crosses the twenty two metres line and is then blown back, play shall continue.

3. If the ball pitches directly into touch, the opposing team may accept the kick, have the ball dropped out again, or have a scrummage formed at the centre of the twenty two metres line.

4. The *kicker's team* must be behind the ball when kicked; otherwise a scrummage shall be formed at the centre of the twenty two metres line.

5. The *opposing team* must not charge over the twenty-two metres line; otherwise the ball shall be dropped out again.

# LAW 15

Unlike a kick off from the centre line, a drop-out from the twenty two can be taken anywhere along the line so long as the kick is taken from behind the line. If the player kicking the ball crosses the line while taking the kick, he shall retake the kick. There is no option to the non-offending side. Similarly, if the wrong type of kick is taken, for example a punt instead of a drop kick, the kick shall be retaken properly.

If, once the kick has been taken, the ball does not cross the twenty two-metres line the other side have the option of the kick being retaken or a scrummage. If the scrummage is opted for, it shall be formed at the centre of the twenty-two metres line with the attacking side putting the ball in. It should be noted that the scrum is always set at the centre irrespective of where the original drop-out was taken. As with other aspects of this law, the advantage law can be applied by the referee, if appropriate. In other words if the ball does not cross the line and the attacking side play the ball and score a try or end up in a more advantageous position, the referee should allow play to continue. Obviously if the ball crosses the twenty-two metres line and is blown back, play should be allowed to continue.

If the ball is kicked directly into touch, the opposing team have the choice of three options as detailed in the law. Firstly, the kick can be retaken. Secondly, a scrummage can be chosen again to be formed at the centre of the twenty-two metres line or thirdly, the kick can be accepted. If the last option is chosen, a line-out is the award and because the drop-out was taken from behind the twenty-two metres line, the position of the line-out shall be where the ball crossed the touch line.

When the drop-out is taken, the kicker's team must be behind the kicker. If they are not there is no option but a scrummage at the centre of the twenty two metre line with the attacking side putting the ball in. Again, the referee might be able to allow advantage before awarding the scrum.

If a drop-out is to be taken, the opposing team are allowed to charge the kick down as long as they do not cross the twenty two metre line in their attempt to do so. If they do, the kick shall be retaken. Referees should always be aware of a quick-drop-out being attempted by the defending team. If the defending team are prevented by the opposition from taking a quick drop-out either by obstruction of the ball carrier as he is running up to the twenty two or by a player staying on the wrong side of the twenty-two metres line and interfering with the kicker, the referee should award a penalty. If a penalty is awarded by the referee, the mark is anywhere along the twenty-two metres line at the option of the defending team. This is due to the fact that the drop-out can be taken at any position along the line therefore any resultant penalty must be where the ball would next be brought into play. The referee should indicate the award at the centre of the line but thereafter, the kicker can opt for any position along the line.

# LAW 16
## *Fair-Catch (Mark)*

A  A player makes a fair-catch when being stationary with both feet on the ground, in his twenty two metres area or in his In-goal, he cleanly catches the ball direct from a kick, knock-on or throw-forward by one of this opponents and, at the same time, he exclaims 'Mark!' A fair-catch may be obtained even though the ball on its way touches a goal post or crossbar and can be made in In-goal.

B  A free kick is awarded for a fair-catch.

1.  The kick must be taken by the player making the fair-catch, unless he is injured in so doing. If he is unable to take the kick within one minute a scrummage shall be formed at the mark. His team shall put in the ball.

2.  If the mark is in In-goal, any resultant scrummage shall be five metres from the goal line on a line through the mark.

# LAW 16

Before awarding a fair-catch or a mark, the referee must ensure that the player is stationary, with *both* feet on the ground, that he catches the ball cleanly i.e. without dropping it or knocking it on and calls 'mark' simultaneously. If any of the above do or do not happen, play should be allowed to continue.

As is explained in the introduction to the actual law, a mark can be made not only directly from a kick by the opposition, but from a pass or knock-on. Similarly, although a mark has to be made directly from an opponent, that is, without the ball touching another player, referee or the ground, a mark can still be awarded if the ball rebounds from the crossbar or goal post, for example following a penalty kick at goal.

As previously explained in Law 14, a mark can be made in In-goal and the kick must be taken from that mark.

If a mark or fair-catch is made correctly, a free kick is awarded. See Law 28.

Unlike a free kick for a technical infringement, which can be taken by any member of the team awarded the free kick, a free kick awarded for a mark must only be taken by the person making the mark. If a player is injured in making the mark and cannot take the kick, then the referee should award a scrummage with the kicker's team putting the ball in. If the mark is made In-goal and the kick cannot be taken the scrum has to be formed five metres from the goal line on a line through the mark but no closer to the touch line than five metres.

It should noted that the only time a scrummage is the award for a free kick or mark is when the player making the mark is injured and cannot take the kick. There is no choice, as there is in Law 28, for the kicker's team to choose the scrum in preference to the kick.

Players should be aware that referees will penalise them if they unfairly charge the catcher after the referee has blown his whistle for a fair-catch. A penalty kick would then be the award.

## LAW 17
### *Knock-On or Throw-Forward*

A knock-on occurs when the ball travels forward towards the direction of the opponents' dead-ball line after:
— a player loses possession of it, or
— a player propels or strikes it with his hand or arm, or
— it strikes a player's hand or arm.

A throw-forward occurs when a player carrying the ball throws or passes it in the direction of his opponents' dead-ball line. A throw-in from touch is not a throw-forward. If the ball is not thrown or passed forward but it bounces forward after hitting a player or the ground, it it not a throw-forward.

1. The knock-on or throw-forward must not be *intentional*.

2. If the knock-on or throw-forward is *unintentional*, a scrummage shall be formed either at the place of infringement or, if it occurs at a line-out, fifteen metres from the touch line along the line-of-touch unless:
— a fair catch has been allowed, or
— the ball is knocked on by a player who is in the act of charging down the kick of an opponent but is not attempting to catch the ball, or
— the ball is knocked on one or more times by a player who is in the act of catching or picking it up or losing possession of it and is recovered by that player before it has touched the ground or another player.

## LAW 17

One of the important things to learn from this law is that for a knock-on to have taken place, the ball must have gone in a forward direction and either come in contact with the ground or another player. The player the ball comes in contact with can be from either side. If the ball goes sideways or indeed backwards, bounces and then goes forward this is not a knock-on. Similarly, if a player loses possession of the ball and it drops vertically, bounces and goes forward this is not a knock-on. For the referee to award a knock-on, the ball must in the first instance travel in a forward direction prior to its hitting the ground or another player.

If the ball is knocked forward by a player attempting to charge down an opponent's kick, this is not classified as a knock-on as long as the player charging the ball down is not making an attempt to grasp the ball. It should be noted that in this situation play will continue only if the attempted charge down was of a kick. A charge down of an opponent's pass would be deemed a knock-on if the ball travelled forward.

If the referee deems the knock-on to be unintentional, then he would award a scrummage at the place of infringement. If there was more than one knock-on, then the scrummage would be awarded at the position of the first one. Advantage, of course, should be allowed if possible. Reference should be made to Law 20, the scrummage, regarding the position of any resultant scrummage close to the goal or touch lines.

If the referee deems that the player knocked or threw the ball forward intentionally, then he should award a penalty kick at the place of infringement. He should also be aware that if a defender intentionally knocks the ball forward near his own goal line, a penalty try might be a possible award if a try might have been scored. In coming to his decision whether or not a knock-on or throw-forward is intentional, the referee will have to decide whether the player knocking the ball on was making an attempt to grasp the ball. This can be ascertained by looking at the player's body and hand position, also if his arm is making a downward movement. If he is over-stretching to reach the ball, the chances are that the knock-on is intentional, also if the palms of his hands are facing towards the ground it is more than likely he was making no attempt to grasp the ball. For a throw-forward to be penalised, the player has to have made a deliberate motion to have thrown the ball forward. For example, a player with the ball in his possession throwing the ball forward over an oncoming opponent and catching the ball once he and the ball have passed the opponent would be deemed intentional and be penalised.

Another situation which sometimes causes controversy is when the ball is knocked on by an attacking player and the ball then travels into In-goal where it is made dead. Some years ago, the award was a twenty two metre drop-out due to the fact that the referee had played advantage. This has since been changed and now a scrum would be awarded in the field-of-play at the place of infringement with the defending team have the put in. It was felt that the drop-out was too much of an advantage hence this alteration was introduced. A similar award is given if the ball goes forward and travels into In-goal after having touched an opponent who does not wilfully attempt to stop, catch or kick it and the ball is made dead. The referee has to decide whether or not the defending player made an attempt to touch the ball or whether the ball 'played the player'.

A knock-on can occur in the In-goal area and reference should be made to Law 14 to ascertain the position of a resultant award.

# LAW 18
## *Tackle, Lying With, on or Near the Ball*

A tackle occurs when a player carrying the ball in the field-of-play is held by one or more opponents so that while he is so held he is brought to the ground or the ball comes into contact with the ground. If the ball carrier is on one knee, or both knees, or is sitting on the ground, or is on top of another player who is on the ground, the ball carrier is deemed to have been brought to the ground.

1.  a.  A tackled player *must immediately* pass the ball or release the ball *and* get up move or away from the ball.

    b.  A player who goes to the ground and gathers the ball or with the ball in his possession but who is not tackled *must immediately* get up on his feet with the ball *or* pass the ball *or* release the ball and get up or move away from the ball.

    c.  Any other player must be on his feet before he can play.

2.  It is illegal for any player:

    a.  to prevent a tackled player from passing or releasing the ball, or getting up or moving away after he has passed or released it,

ILLEGAL PLAY ON THE GROUND:- The player with the dark jersey is on the ground holding onto the ball and so preventing the scrum half in the lighter jersey, who is on his feet, playing the ball. Law 18 (1c) and (2c).

   b. to pull the ball from a tackled player's possession or attempt to pick up the ball before the tackled player has released it,

   c. while lying on the ground after a tackle to play or interfere with the ball in any way or to tackle or attempt to tackle an opponent carrying the ball,

   d. to wilfully fall on or over a player lying on the ground with the ball in his possession,

   e. to wilfully fall on or over players lying on the ground with the ball between them or in close proximity, or,

   f. while lying on the ground in close proximity to the ball to prevent an opponent from gaining possession of it.

3. A player must not fall on or over the ball emerging from a scrummage or ruck.

4. A try may be scored if the momentum of a player carries him into his opponents' In-goal even though he is tackled.

Passing the ball immediately when tackled

# LAW 18

It has been stressed before and cannot be emphasised enough that the game of Rugby Football is for players on their feet. It is therefore important that the main law – Law 18 – pertaining to the tackle, laying with, on or near the ball is understood by all. The interpretation that should be placed on the requirement for players to be on their feet is that, if a player is on the ground, he is no longer part of the game and can do nothing until he gets to his feet.

The first part of Law 18 concerns the tackle. A tackle is defined as to have taken place when, 'a player carrying the ball in the field-of-play is held by one or more opponents so that while he is so held, he is brought to the ground or the ball comes in contact with the ground.' The definition carries on to explain that if the ball carrier is held and is on one or both knees or is sitting on the ground or on top of players on the ground, that also is a tackle.

The ball must be released or passed immediately when tackled

The important thing to bear in mind is that the ball carrier must be held and must continue to be held until he or the ball come into contact with the ground. The so called 'tap tackle', where the ball carrier is brought to ground by an opponent tapping his ankles and not by holding him is not a tackle neither is it a tackle, as it was some years ago, if the ball carrier is held or is lifted off the ground by an opponent.

Once a player has been correctly tackled, he must comply with the law *immediately*. He must either pass or release the ball *and* get up or move away from the ball. A player is allowed to pass the ball as he is falling to ground in the tackle or when he or the ball hits the ground, so long as the pass is made immediately the ball or player hits the ground. Referees should be strict in penalising tackled players on the ground who hold on to the ball too long because this invariably leads to unwanted 'pile-ups' and the possibility of players on the ground being injured. If the tackled player chooses not to pass

Even when tackled, a player can stretch for the goal line

the ball he must release the ball immediately he is tackled. The requirements to release the ball allows a player to place the ball on the ground in any direction, including forward, or to throw the ball or push it along the ground provided, in this case, it is not in a forward direction.

Once a tackled player has complied with the law pertaining to passing or releasing, many players think that that is that. It is essential that if the ball is placed close to the tackle situation, the tackled player must attempt to get up or move away from the ball. Obviously there are certain times because of the speed of the game and with other players arriving quickly after a tackle, that it is impossible for the tackled player to move and referees should take notice of this fact in their decisions. If time does allow for a tackled player to move or get up he should do so immediately or a penalty kick will be awarded against him.

There are two instances when a tackled player need not pass or release the ball immediately in a tackle. These instances

A tackled player must get to his feet before he can play again

occur close to the try line. Firstly if the momentum of a player, when tackled, carries him into his opponent's In-goal he can be awarded a score, even if the tackle occurred some way short of the line. Secondly, if the tackle occurs short of the goal line and the tackled player can stretch his arm and place the ball on or over the line a try can be awarded. In the second case, it should be emphasised that it must be a movement with the arm only, any other will be liable to be penalised. The situation where a player is tackled short of the line but is still able to make another movement in an attempt to score a try still may look wrong in a lot of people's eyes, but in law it can be acceptable.

Now let us look at the actions of the tackler and what he can or cannot do in the tackle.

The law clearly states that it is illegal for any player, including the tackler, to prevent the tackled player from releasing the

A player cannot wilfully fall on or over another player

ball. It is also illegal for any player to prevent the tackled player from getting up or moving away after the ball has been passed or released. In other words, once a player has made a successful tackle, he cannot remain lying on top or over his opponent, neither can he continue to grasp the tackled player and by so doing prevent him from getting up or from moving away from the ball. In many cases, it is the tackled player who is wrongly penalised for not releasing the ball and moving away when, in reality, he cannot comply with the law because the tackler, by his illegal actions, prevents him from doing so.

The onus is firstly on the tackled player to comply with the law and thereafter on the tackler. The notes to this section of the law indicate that if the referee is in doubt as to responsibility for failure to pass or release the ball, he should *at once* order a scrummage. (Reference should be made to Law 20 to determine which side puts the ball in.) There are therefore certain occasions where referees appear to blow up a situation quicker than players and spectators would wish. This is not because of the ineptitude of the referee but due to the fact that the body positions of the tackler and the tackled player trap the ball and make it impossible for the ball to be released or played. To allow such a situation to develop might cause injury to the players on the ground or would lead to the inevitable 'pile-up' which legislators are trying to remove from the game.

Let us now assume that the tackler has complied with the law insofar as that he has not prevented the tackled player from passing or releasing the ball or from getting up or moving away from the ball. What precisely can he do? The simple answer is nothing. If he remains on the ground after a tackle he is out of the game and cannot take part again until he gets to his feet. He is not allowed to play or interfere in any way with the ball. He cannot intentionally touch the ball even if it is firstly played by an opponent. If an opponent, on his feet, picks up the ball, a tackler, who is still on the ground, cannot tackle or attempt to tackle the ball carrier as was the case a few seasons ago.

It is not only the players involved in the tackle, ie the tackled player and the tackler or tacklers, who must comply with the tackle law, but the players from both sides who are next to the tackle situation.

It is illegal for any player, including the tackler, to pull the ball from the tackled player's possession or attempt to pick up the ball before the tackled player has released it. Obviously, if the tackled player complies with his section of the law and releases the ball immediately he is tackled, it would be very unusual for a player to be penalised for trying to pull the ball from a tackled player before that tackled player has released it. The one exception allowed in law in this situation is the one mentioned earlier, where a tackled player, short of the goal line, can attempt to place the ball over the line and score a try. In such circumstances any defending player, including the tackler, may attempt to prevent a try being scored by pulling the ball from the ball carrier's possession. He is only allowed to pull the ball from the hands of the player *not* kick the ball out of the player's hands. If in such circumstances the defending player did kick the ball from the attacking player's possession a penalty try would probably be awarded by the referee.

By far the greatest number of penalties awarded by referees under Law 18 is for players on their feet falling on or over tackled players. The law again is very specific. It is illegal for *any* player to wilfully fall on or over players lying on the ground with the ball between them or in close proximity to them. Close proximity is defined in the law as being within one metre.

Assuming the tackled player and the tackler have complied with the law but the ball is either lying between them or lying within one metre of where they are lying, it is illegal for any player to fall wilfully on or over the players on the ground. People assume that a player can go to ground in this situation so long as he plays the ball before he actually comes in contact with the ground or with the players on the ground, but this is not the case. If this happens a penalty should be awarded. The only things players can do in this situation are to pick the ball up or drive over the ball or stand over the ball and create a platform for a ruck to form. It should be noted that in driving over the ball players are allowed to go beyond the ball by one step before coming into contact with the opposition. If the player drives more than one step beyond the ball he is liable to be penalised for obstruction. If the ball is lying free from the players on the ground on the side of team A, but still within one metre of the tackle, a player from team A can go to ground to play the ball as long as he complies with the law and does not come into contact with the players on the ground.

The law states that players should not *wilfully* fall on or over players etc. It is up to the referee to decide whether or not players wilfully go to ground or whether because of circumstances, for example no opposition to ruck against or tripping up over players on the ground they accidentally end up over tackled players on the ground. If the referee deems that players go to ground unintentionally he should award a scrum unless the ball can be played immediately by the scrum half.

The last part of Law 18 deals with the player who is not tackled, but who goes to ground either with the ball in his possession or with the intention of gathering a loose ball which is already on the ground.

Examples of players who come within this section of the law could be, for instance, a full back who falls on the ground to secure a loose ball or a player, who having the ball in his possession, is 'ankle tapped' by an opponent and falls to the ground although not tackled.

In these two examples, Law 18 is very specific as to the obligations placed upon the player. Such a player on the ground must *immediately*:

1. get up on his feet with the ball *or*
2. pass the ball *or*
3. release the ball **and** get up or move away from the ball.

Unlike when a player is tackled, if a player does go to ground in the circumstances described above he does have the option to get to his feet with the ball in his possession so long as he does so immediately.

Assuming that the player on the ground with the ball in his possession does not get to his feet what other options are open to him? Well he can pass the ball to a colleague, but again, he must do so immediately and not put off time waiting for a team mate to arrive before passing. Any such delay by the man on the ground will be subject to penalty. Once he has passed the ball, the player is out of the game until he gets to his feet. He cannot play the ball again while he is still on the ground, neither can he attempt to tackle an opponent who may have won possession of the ball nor prevent an opponent from gaining possession of the ball.

The other option available to a player with the ball in his possession is for him to release the ball while he is still on the ground. It might be that a forward goes to ground to secure the ball and because of tactics he wishes his fellow forwards to ruck over himself and the ball. In such circumstances it must be pointed out, that the player on the ground who releases the ball cannot then lie near to the ball. The law, as has already been stated, emphasises the point that once a player has released the ball he *must* make an effort to get up or move away from it. Obviously there are certain situations, due to the speed of the game and the proximity of players, when a player on the ground has no time to move before players start to ruck over both himself and the ball. In these circumstances the player should not be penalised as long as he does not interfere with the ball being played by players of either team who are on their feet. As with the player who passes the ball, a player who releases the ball cannot play the ball again and cannot tackle or interfere with an opponent until he is on his feet.

If a player goes to ground to secure the ball or is on the ground with the ball in his possession what options are open to an opponent? The law states that it is illegal for any player to:

> '. . . *wilfully fall on or over a player on the ground with the ball in his possession*'

This means that an opposition player cannot fall on top of a player who is on the ground holding the ball. In fact, an opposition player must allow the ball carrier to regain his feet before he can tackle him. If the ball carrier is in the process of regaining his feet he cannot be tackled by an opponent until he is fully supported by both feet. Obviously the ball carrier must get to his feet immediately or he will be penalised.

After dealing with the tackle and with players going to ground with the ball or to secure or gather the ball, the law continues by stating that:

> '*Any other player must be on his feet before he can play*'

This was a major alteration to the law which previously had stated that any other player had to be on his feet before he could play the ball. The words 'the ball' being omitted.

Basically this means that if any player, other than the ones mentioned previously, are not on their feet ie they are lying or kneeling on the ground, they are out of the game. They cannot play the ball, tackle an opponent or interfere with an opponent trying to gather the ball. The guideline to follow is:

> *If you are on the ground you are out of the game*

and you cannot take further part in the game until you are back on your feet.

# LAW 19
## *Lying With, on or Near the Ball*

This particular law which refers to a player lying with, on or near the ball was incorporated into law 18 some years ago. There is no longer a law 19, but instead of renumbering all the subsequent laws, the actual number remains within the law book.

# LAW 20
## *Scrummage*

A scrummage, which can take place only in the field-of-play, is formed by players from each team closing up in readiness to allow the ball to be put on the ground between them but is not to be formed within five metres of the touch line.

The middle player in each front row is the hooker, and the players on either side of him are the props.

The middle line means an imaginary line on the ground directly beneath the line formed by the junction of the shoulders of the two front rows.

If the ball in a scrummage is on or over the goal line the scrummage is ended.

### Forming a Scrummage

1. A team must not wilfully delay the forming of a scrummage.

2. Every scrummage shall be formed at the place of infringement or as near thereto as is practicable within the field-of-play. It must be stationary with the middle line parallel to the goal lines until the ball has been put in.
   Before commencing engagement, each front row must be in a crouched position with heads and shoulders no lower than their hips and so that they are not more than one arm's length from the opponents' shoulders.
   In the interests of safety each front row should touch on the upper arms and then pause prior to engagement in the sequence: crouch – touch – pause – engage.

3. It is dangerous play for a front row to form down some distance from its opponents and rush against them.

4. A minimum of five players from each team shall be required to form a scrummage. While the scrummage is in progress a minimum of five players shall remain bound in the scrummage until it ends. Each front row of a scrummage shall have three players in it *at all times*. The head of a player in a front row shall not be next to the head of a player of the same team.

5. a. While a scrummage is forming:
  — the shoulders of each player in the front row must not
    be lower than his hips.
  — all players in each front row must adopt a normal
    stance.
  — both feet must be on the ground and not crossed.
  — the hookers must be in a hooking position.
  — a hooker's foot must not be in front of the forward
    feet of his props.

  b. While the scrummage is taking place, players in each front
    row must have their weight firmly on at least one foot and be
    in a position for an effective forward shove and the shoulders
    of each player must not be lower than his hips.

  c. When five players of a team form the scrummage the two
    players in the second row must remain bound to each other
    until the scrummage ends.

LEGAL SCRUMMAGE PLAY:- Once the ball is on or over the goal line the scrummage is
ended, Law 20. Here the scrum half dived legally into a scrummage to score a try after
the ball had touched the goal line.

## Binding of Players

6. a. The players of each front row shall bind firmly and continuously while the scrummage if forming, while the ball is being put in and while it is in the scrummage.

   b. The hooker may bind either over or under the arms of his props but, in either case, he must bind firmly around their bodies at or below the level of the armpits. The props must bind the hooker similarly. The hooker must not be supported so that he is not carrying any weight on either foot.

   c. The outside (loose-head) prop *must* either (i) bind his opposing (tight-head) prop with his left arm inside the right arm of his opponent, or (ii) place his left hand or forearm on his left thigh.

      The tight-head prop *must* bind with his right arm outside the left upper arm of his opposing loose-head prop. He may

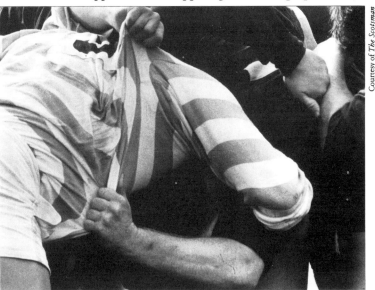

Courtesy of *The Scotsman*

ILLEGAL BINDING IN THE SCRUMMAGE:- Tight head prop (hooped jersey) pushing down on opponent, while loose head prop (plain coloured jersey) is pulling down on opponent's jersey. Law 20 (6c).

grip the jersey of his opposing loose-lead prop with his right hand but only to keep himself and the scrummage steady and he must not exert a downward pull.

d. All players in a scrummage, other than those in a front row, must bind with at least one arm and hand around the body of another player of the same team.

e. No outside player other than a prop may hold an opponent with his outer arm.

### Putting the Ball into the Scrummage

7. When an infringement occurs the team not responsible shall put in the ball. In other circumstances, unless otherwise provided, the ball shall be put in by the team which was moving forward prior to the stoppage or, if neither team was moving forward, by the attacking team.

8. The ball shall be put in without delay as soon as the two front rows have closed together. A team must put in the ball when ordered to do so and on the side first chosen.

9. The player putting in the ball shall:

a. stand one metre from the scrummage and midway between the two front rows.

b. hold the ball with both hands midway between the two front rows at a level midway between his knee and ankle.

c. from that position put in the ball:

— without any delay or without feint or backward movement, i.e. with a single forward movement, and

— at a quick speed straight along the middle line so that it first touches the ground immediately beyond the width of the nearer prop's shoulders.

10. Play in the scrummage begins when the ball leaves the hands of the player putting it in.

11. If the ball is put in and it comes out at either end of the tunnel, it shall be put in again, unless a free kick or penalty kick has been awarded.

If the ball comes out other than at either end of the tunnel and if a penalty kick has not been awarded play shall proceed.

### Restrictions on Front Row Players

12. All front row players must place their feet so as to allow a clear tunnel. A player must not prevent the ball from being put into the scrummage, or from touching the ground at the required place.

13. No front row player may raise or advance a foot until the ball has touched the ground.

14. When the ball has touched the ground, any foot of any player in either front row may be used in an attempt to gain possession of the ball subject to the following:
    players in the front rows must not *at any time* during the scrummage:
    a. raise both feet off the ground at the same time, or
    b. wilfully adopt any position or wilfully take any action, by twisting or lowering the body or by pulling on an opponent's dress, which is likely to cause the scrummage to collapse, or
    c. wilfully kick the ball out of the tunnel in the direction from which it was put in.

### Restrictions on Players

15. Any player who is not in either front row must not play the ball while it is in the tunnel.

16. A player must not:
    a. return the ball into the scrummage, or
    b. handle the ball in the scrummage except in the act of obtaining a ('push-over') try to touch-down, or
    c. pick up the ball in the scrummage by hand or legs, or
    d. wilfully collapse the scrummage, or
    e. wilfully fall or kneel in the scrummage, or
    f. attempt to gain possession of the ball in the scrummage with any part of the body except the foot or lower leg.

17. The player putting in the ball and his immediate opponent must not kick the ball while it is in the scrummage.

18. A scrummage must not be wheeled beyond a position where the middle line becomes parallel to the touch line. The scrummage will be reformed at the site of the stoppage, the ball to be put in by the side that has gained possession or otherwise by the same team.

# LAW 20

A scrum can arise from just about any other facet of play, such as a kick-off, restart kick, line-out, ruck, maul not to mention the obvious knock-on or forward pass.

Each scrum must have a minimum of five players from each team and the front row shall have three players in it at all times. The setting of the scrum must always be in the field-of-play at least five metres from touch and if it is near a goal line it must be positioned in such a way that the feet of the front and second rows of the defending side are in the field-of-play.

Let us look, firstly, at the formation of the scrum. Having set the mark for the scrum the referee will keep the two front rows apart until the putting in scrum half arrives with the ball at the tunnel of the scrum. Then both front rows should be in a crouched position at arms length ready to engage in the sequence: crouch – touch – pause – engage. Apart from the touch aspect most front row players are happy with that sequence and most referees are also willing to forego touching as long as the other stipulations are adhered to. If a team, usually in the shape of a prop, wilfully delay the forming of a scrummage, then that team will be penalised. A penalty will also be awarded when a front row forms down some distance from its opponents and rushes against them, as this is dangerous play.

Now, after engagement, the binding of the forwards must be as follows, otherwise penalties will result against the offenders:

- a. Hooker
    - i.    over the shoulders and round the bodies of his props – or
    - ii.   under the shoulders and round the bodies of his props – or
    - iii.  either over or under the shoulders and round the bodies of his props, ie one over and one under.
    - iv.   continuously and tightly. No loose arms and slipping the bind, slipping round the neck of his props.
- b. Props as above, i, ii and iii. There must be no slipping of binding on the hooker to allow the hooker more freedom.
- c. No other player can bind on to an opponent. Which

The hooker must bind correctly with no slipping of binding

includes wing forwards slipping forward and binding on to the opposition props.

The binding on the opposite front row must be so that the tight-head prop's arm is outside that of the opposing loose-head prop. Each may grip each others jersey to keep themselves steady *not* to pull each other down.

No angled packing (boring in). Everybody pushing forward. The level – height of the front row's shoulders should not be below the level of the hips.

However, allowances will be made for height difference between individual opponents, ground conditions, dry or firm, wet and slippery and the fact that a scrum is not a rigid formation.

Whilst the tight-head prop must bind with his right arm outside the left upper arm of his opposing loose-head prop, (he may grip the jersey of his opposing loose-head prop with his right hand but only to keep himself and the srummage steady and he must not exert a downward pull), the loose-head prop may use his outside arm on his leg to support himself. Feet position – normal stance, both on the ground in a forward pushing position. Again as the scrum is a dynamic event, these positions will alter and vary depending again on many factors:
   a. ground conditions
   b. comparative sizes of the packs
   c. whether it is an attacking or defensive scrum

The hooker's body and feet positions are slightly different. No twisting of the hips and shoulders to extremes although a little leeway has to be allowed because of the mechanics of hooking. His feet must be behind his loose-head's outside foot, not in front of his own shoulders thus keeping the tunnel clear and there must be no lowering or dipping of the hips. All these tend to make the scrum loose and liable to collapse.

What may happen when the ball is in the scrum?

The scrum half has the ball in both hands standing an arm's length from the tunnel, standing on the midline of the scrum not the centre of the tunnel. The midline is directly below the join of shoulders of the two front rows. Once the scrum half has brought the ball below the knee but above the ankle, he should put the ball in without delay, with a feint or backward movement at quick speed along the midline beyond the width of his loose-head prop's shoulder. This is the ideal, and in practice slight leeway has to be allowed because of the dynamic nature of the scrum.

A delayed put in can create problems, eg instability or friction between front rows or opposing scrum halves.

If there is a delay by the scrum half, he will be ordered to put the ball in, *if that advice is ignored* a free kick will be awarded for the delay.

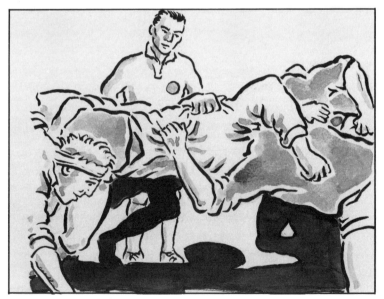

Props must not pull down

Once the ball has left the scrum half's hands, the scrum has started. If the ball goes through the scrum and out the other side, or straight back out without infringement, the ball will be put in again.

Referees at this time will be looking at possible penable offences such as:

a. foot up by props preventing the ball getting into the scrum and whether it is a repeated infringement.
b. early strike by hookers, although advantage will be played if the non-offending side wins the ball.
c. ball chasing by hooker into the opposing scrum with both feet.
d. altering binding (known as twisting/lowering) to secure his own ball.
e. wing forwards putting their feet into the tunnel to help win the ball.

When the ball has been won fairly and is travelling through the scrum, what will referees be looking for and where?

By the ball-winning side:

a. any returning of the ball into the scrum.
b. any helping back of the ball by hand.
c. wing forward swinging out from his original position to obstruct the other scrum half following the ball.

By the other side:

a. disruption by pulling jerseys to wheel the scrum.
b. wing forwards creeping forward, especially on the far side of the scrum.
c. scrum half kicking the ball while in the scrum.
d. scrum half leaning or using a wing forward to gain leverage to interfere with his opponent.
e. checking backs for off-side.

What about scrums near goal lines?

Firstly, with attacking possession, the referee must try at all times to have sight of the ball. In a push-over attempt, he concentrates on the ball, the players close to the ball and the proximity of the goal line.

The points a referee looks for are early 'diving in' of the defending side, off-side by defenders and collapsing of scrum. The referee should award a penalty although if he decides that but for foul play a try would in all probability have been scored then a penalty try would be awarded.

In the case of defending possession, the ball is not as important as the attacking players trying to prevent clearance by the defenders eg

    a. creeping forward by far-side attacking wing forward.
    b. interference of the defending scrum half by his immediate opponent.
    c. attacking backs getting a 'flyer' ie from an off-side position to pressure the defenders.

A scrum has ended when the ball has cleared the back feet of the scrummage, generally the No 8's feet. As long as the No 8's feet are covering the ball, it is still in the scrum. Remember that if the No 8 has his head out of the second row and is hanging on to their shorts, the ball is out, the No 8 is not properly bound. In that circumstance, the opposition can help themselves to the ball, without penalty!

With a wheeling scrum referees tend to watch the side without the ball more closely. The wheel appears to be a negative, defensive and destructive move in the modern game to spoil possession, thus spoiling the chance of good positive play.

If the scrum goes past 90° and there is no intentional wheel, the laws now state that the referee must order a re-scrummage at the site of stoppage with the side in possession putting the ball into the re-scrummage.

The collapsed scrum is the most spectacular, dangerous and controversial happening in the scrum. It is also the most difficult facet to referee correctly and fairly.

The referee should ask himself, (a) why collapse a scrum? (b) how does a scrum collapse?

- a. i. one team protecting their own ball when it has been won in a retreating scrum.
  - ii. a side being driven back in scrum, preventing advance of the ball-winning team, by collapsing.
  - iii. to con the referee in hope of getting a penalty.
- b. i. loose binding and bad position of bodies.
  - ii. slipping binding by props.
  - iii. boring in by props.
  - iv. pulling down by props.
  - v. forcing down by props.

It is very difficult to decide who is responsible. Should a referee penalise the tight-head because he is bigger, heavier and stronger than the opposing loose-head who cannot seem to take the legal pressure? Did the loose-head slip his binding or

No 8 is still correctly bound – ball is still in the scrummage

was the opposing tight-head exerting the pressure illegally by forcing his opponents shoulders below the level of his hips?

Things that referees should take into consideration:
  a. state of ground – firm and dry or wet and soft.
  b. time in the game – very early when scrums have not yet
     settled down; Very late when tiredness is a factor.
  c. position in the field – more often near goal lines.
  d. who's put in – defender or attacker. Is it always likely to be only the defenders who collapse the scrum although the referee should be aware of attackers trying to win a kickable penalty.
  e. delay in putting in the ball.
  f. physical size of the opposing scrums.

Near-side collapses are much easier to referee than far-side ones. Referees should go round to the other side if they have far-side collapses to try and sort out the problem eg adjusting the binding, speaking to the players, letting them know that they will be penalised. Quick collapses in general are accidental ie the scrum just caves in with nobody in particular to blame. If it is accidental and it caves in, the referee should blow up immediately on the grounds of safety, and order a re-scrum – no matter where the ball is in the original scrum.

There is no easy answer, and sometimes, in making a decision, probability comes into it as well as absolute certainty.

But if a referee has to penalise on probability then he should!

Collapsing scrums are dangerous and must be prevented in the first place and stopped if they happen.

If a prop is 'popped' or lifted the referee, again, on the grounds of safety will blow up and order a re-scrum. This is especially dangerous for the tight-head prop or hooker who has his head and neck wedged between two opponents. The pressure from his own back five forwards pushing one way and the opposing pack pushing the other can lead to disastrous results. If the 'popping' was repeated the referee would be perfectly correct in penalising the offender and in certain circumstances ordering him from the field-of-play.

Having spoken to players and coaches alike they appreciate an immediate, quick whistle by the referee to avoid serious injury to any player.

# LAW 21
## *Ruck*

A ruck, which can take place only in the field-of-play, is formed when the ball is on the ground and one or more players from each team are on their feet and in physical contact, closing around the ball between them.

If the ball in a ruck is on or over the goal line the ruck is ended.

1.  A player joining a ruck must have his head and shoulders no lower than his hips. He must bind with at least one arm around the body of a player of his team in the ruck.

2.  A player must not:
    a.  return the ball into the ruck, or
    b.  handle the ball in the ruck except in the act of securing a try or touch-down, or
    c.  pick up the ball in the ruck by hand or legs, or
    d.  wilfully collapse the ruck, or

A properly formed ruck

e. jump on top of other players in the ruck, or

f. wilfully fall or kneel in the ruck, or

g. while lying on the ground interfere in any way with the ball in or emerging from the ruck. He must do his best to roll away from it.

# LAW 21

Unlike the maul (see Law 22), a ruck can be formed with only two players so long as the players are from different sides. The term 'rucking' is well used in today's game and sometimes people mistake 'rucking' for a ruck being formed and expect the laws of the ruck to be applied. The term 'rucking' is usually meant to imply one team either playing the ball back with their feet or in most cases one team driving over the ball to engage the other team and by so doing leaving the ball clear and available for their scrum half to pick up. Unless the team driving over the ball engage the opposition directly over the ball, while still on their feet, no ruck is formed according to the definition, and therefore the laws of the ruck pertaining to offside etc do not apply. Many times in today's game this situation occurs and players and spectators alike get upset because the referee has not penalised a player for being offside at the ruck when in reality no ruck ever existed.

*A ruck can only take place in the field-of-play.* This is similar to the laws regarding the scrummage and the maul. Once the ball is on or has crossed the goal line the ruck has ended and players from either side can attempt to fall on the ball in order to ground it. As with the scrummage, players should not be allowed to dive into a ruck before the ball crosses the line or else a penalty try could be awarded against the offending player or players.

*The ruck ends when the ball emerges from it.* Again this is similar to the scrummage. Once the whole of the ball has emerged from the ruck and can be picked up by a player not in the ruck, the ruck is ended. Once the ball has emerged it cannot be returned into a ruck by any player. A free kick will be awarded for this infringement. Nothing is laid down in law explaining exactly when a ball has emerged from a ruck. Every referee will have a slight variation in interpretation as to whether a ball is in or out of a ruck, but the large majority will say that so long as there is no part of a player's body directly above the ball, then it is out. Scrum halves who are attempting to pick the ball up must not be allowed to 'burrow' into the ruck to obtain the ball but must wait until the ball is clear before picking it up. A penalty kick at the place of infringement is the award for infringement.

Assuming a ruck has been formed correctly, let us look at the players' options and what the referee is looking for.

*Once a ruck has formed, a player joining the ruck must have his head and shoulders no lower than his hips.* This is similar to the maul and is an attempt to prevent injury due to bad body positioning. A free kick at the place of infringement is the award here. Very few free kicks are awarded in the game for this infringement, not because referees are ignoring the law but because most referees are too busy looking at other things happening as a ruck is forming.

*A player joining a ruck must bind with at least one arm around the body of a player of his own team already in the ruck.* Binding involves having at least one arm, that is from hand to shoulder, around the body of a team-mate. Merely placing the hand or part of the arm, up to say the elbow, is not sufficient. It is imperative that referees ensure that players are properly bound and are not holding on with one hand hoping to make a quick break in order to tackle the ball carrier. Again a free kick is the award.

*A player must not:*
> — *handle the ball in a ruck or*
> — *pick up the ball in the ruck by hands legs or*
> — *wilfully collapse a ruck or*
> — *wilfully fall or kneel in the ruck or*
> — *jump on top of other players in the ruck or*
> — *while lying on the ground interfere in any way with the ball*

A penalty kick will be awarded for any of the above six infringements. Once the ruck has formed players must use their best endeavours to remain on their feet. If the referee deems that a player wilfully goes to ground in an attempt to secure the ball he will award a penalty. Similarly if a player is on the ground and the ruck forms over him the player on the ground is not allowed to interfere with the ball in any way and in fact must do his best to get away from the ball. This is sometimes difficult to do if a ruck forms quickly over a man on the ground and referees must ensure that the player on the ground is not illegally kicked.

*The off-side line at the ruck means a line parallel to the goal line through the hindmost foot of the player's team in the ruck.*

A player not participating in the ruck must always be behind the off-side line. Like the maul, the scrum half cannot follow the ball round the ruck but must remain behind the off-side line.

*While a ruck is taking place a player is off-side if he:*
> — *joins from his opponent's side or*
> — *joins in front of the ball or*
> — *advances in front of the off-side line or*
> — *does not join the ruck and does not retire behind the off-side line or*
> — *unbinds from the ruck, and does not immediately rejoin it correctly or retire behind the off-side line*

For the above five infringements a penalty kick will be awarded at the place of infringement. It is imperative that referees are strict in ensuring the off-side lines are adhered to. Nothing infuriates players more than if a good ball is won and a player is prevented from playing the ball as he would wish because of a player or players being off-side. Referees must establish the off-side laws early in the game, communicate them to the players and enforce them consistently, throughout the game.

# LAW 22
## *Maul*

A maul, which can take place only in the field-of-play, is formed by one or more players from each team on their feet and in physical contact closing round a player who is carrying the ball.

A maul ends when the ball is on the ground or the ball or a player carrying it emerges from the maul or when a scrummage is ordered.

If the ball in a maul is on or over the goal line the maul is ended.

1.  A player joining a maul must have his head and shoulders no lower than his hips.

2.  A player is not in physical contact unless he is caught in or bound to the maul and not merely alongside it.

3.  A player must not:
    a.  jump on top of players in a maul

PROPERLY FORMED MAUL:- Players from both sides bound together around the ball carrier, Law 22.

    b. wilfully collapse a maul

    c. attempt to drag another player out of a maul

4. When the ball in a maul becomes unplayable a scrummage shall be ordered and the team which was moving forward immediately prior to the stoppage shall put in the ball, or if neither team was moving forward, the attacking team shall put it in.

# LAW 22

It takes at least one player from each side round the ball carrier to form a maul. Certain times in a game what appears to be a maul occurs, but actually is not a maul. What is loosely termed a 'rolling maul' in today's language might not necessarily be a

Courtesy of *The Scotsman*

COLLAPSED MAUL:- If a maul collapses, the referee should award a scrummage unless the ball can be played immediately. Here the maul has collapsed, but the ball is available therefore play can continue. Law 22.

maul and therefore the laws of the maul may not apply. If we take, for example, a situation where a team have the ball in their possession and decide that the forwards should drive the ball on. If the forwards drive on as one body but without any member of the opposition team in physical contact with the actual ball carrier, no maul exists. Similarly, if a player has the ball in his possession and players from the other team bind onto him a maul again has not formed due to the fact that there is only one team bound onto the ball carrier. For a maul to be formed in this situation at least one member of his own team must be bound onto the ball carrier as well.

*A maul can only take place in the field-of-play*. This is similar to the law regarding the scrummage. Once the ball is on or has crossed the goal line the maul has ended and the laws pertaining to the maul can no longer be implemented. There are no longer any off-side lines and players can enter from any direction.

*A maul ends when, in the field-of-play, the ball is placed on or goes to ground. If this occurs a ruck may have formed which is dealt with in Law 21. A maul finishes if a player with the ball emerges from the maul.* There are many occasions in a game when a player with the ball in his possession, although touching the 'maul' with his body but not bound in, dummies to his scrum half in the hope of catching the opposition off-side. Since the maul is no longer in existence we have an open play situation and there is nothing in law to prevent the opposition from attempting to gain the ball.

Assuming a maul has been properly formed, what can the players do and what should the referee be looking for?

A player who subsequently joins a maul, once it is in progress, must have his head and shoulders no lower than his hips. This is to try to prevent serious head and neck injuries due to bad body positioning. A free kick at the place of infringement is the penalty in this situation.

*Players joining a maul must not:*
     *i.   jump on top of players already in the maul or*
     *ii.  wilfully collapse a maul or*
     *iii. attempt to drag another player out of a maul*

The above three instances are punishable by a penalty kick at the place of infringement. In applying the law, once a maul has formed, the referee will not allow any player to pull another player out of the maul either by pulling at his opponent's body or even potentially more dangerous by pulling at his jersey or jersey collar, neither will a referee allow a player to tackle the ball carrier and bring him to the ground. This action is deemed to be wilfully collapsing the maul and will be penalised. Referees should be extremely vigilant in penalising any player who jumps on top of a maul. This can be extremely dangerous both to the players already in the maul and to the player who is doing the jumping.

Once a maul has formed a referee will allow it to continue until the ball becomes unplayable or the maul no longer continues to exist. If a maul collapses and the collapse is not penalised, a referee should order a scrummage unless the ball can be played immediately by a player complying with the laws. The referee will not allow play to continue if the ball becomes trapped in a collapsed maul. In this instance when the maul collapses, the referee should allow the player who is in the scrum half position to pick the ball up. If this player does not pick the ball up immediately, play should be stopped. Referees should not allow a prolonged time for the ball to emerge from a collapsed maul as this results in untidy pile ups and could result in a flash point situation.

Before whistling for a scrummage, the referee should allow a reasonable time for the ball to emerge from the maul, especially if the maul if still moving. Once the maul stops and it is obvious the ball is not going to emerge, the referee should award the scrummage. The referee should not allow prolonged wrestling for the ball.

*The off-side line at the maul means a line parallel to the goal line through the hindmost foot of the player's team in the maul.*

A player not participating in the maul must always be behind the off-side line. It is unlike the scrummage where the scrum half can follow the ball. In the case of the maul the scrum half must be behind the off-side line. If the maul collapses, the referee should still apply the off-side laws as if the maul was still in existence. This way he allows the player in the scrum half position the time required to pick the ball up and play it away from the pile up situation.

When a maul is taking place players who are not in the maul are off-side if they:

    i.   join in front of the ball or

    ii.   join from his opponent's side or

    iii.  do not retire behind the off-side line or

    iv.  advance in front of the off-side line or

    v.   unbind from the maul and do not *immediately* rejoin it behind the ball or retire behind the off-side line.

Referees will be strict in penalising players who creep up in front of the off-side line as this invariably cuts down options for the ball-winning side.

# LAW 23
## *Touch and Line-Out*

## A.   TOUCH
1.  The ball is in touch:
> — when it is not being carried by a player and it touches a touch line or the ground or a person or object on or beyond it, or
> — when it is being carried by a player and it or the player carrying it touches a touch line or the ground beyond it.

2.  If the ball is not in touch and has not crossed the plane of the touch line, a player who is in touch may kick the ball or propel it with his hand but not hold it.

## B.   LINE-OUT
**The line-of-touch is an imaginary line in the field-of-play at right angles to the touch line through the place where the ball is to be thrown in.**

### Formation of Line-out
1.  A line-out is formed by at least two players from each team lining up in single lines parallel to the line-of-touch in readiness for the ball to be thrown in between them. The team throwing in the ball shall determine the maximum number of players from either team who so line up. Such players are those 'in the line-out' unless excluded below.

2.  Until the ball is thrown in each player in the line-out must stand at least one metre from the next player of his team in the line-out, and avoid physical contact with any other player.

3.  The line-out stretches from five metres from the touch line from which the ball is being thrown in, to a position fifteen metres from that touch line.

4.  Any player of either team who is further than fifteen metres from the touch line when the line-out begins is *not* in the line-out.

5. A clear space of 500 mm must be left between the two lines of players.

### Throwing in the Ball

6. When the ball is in touch the place at which it must be thrown in is as follows:

> — when the ball goes into touch from a penalty kick, free kick, or from a kick within twenty two metres of the kicker's goal line, at the place where it touched or crossed the touch line, or
>
> — when the ball pitches directly into touch after having been kicked otherwise than as stated above, opposite the place from which the ball was kicked or at the place where it touched or crossed the touch line if that place be nearer to the kicker's goal line, or
>
> — on all other occasions when the ball is in touch, at the place where it touched or crossed the touch line.

Correct spacing in line-out

In each instance the place is where the ball last crossed the touch line before being in touch.

7. The ball must be thrown in at the line-out by an opponent of the player whom it last touched, or by whom it was carried, before being in touch. In the event of doubt as to which team should throw in the ball, the attacking team shall do so.

8. The ball must be thrown in without delay and without feint.

9. *A quick throw-in* from touch without waiting for the players to form a line-out is permissble provided the ball that went into touch is used, it has been handled only by the players and it is thrown in correctly.

10. The ball may be brought into play by a quick throw-in or at a formed line-out. In either event the player must throw in the ball:

    — at the place indicated, and
    — so that it first touches the ground or touches or is touched by a player at least five metres from the touch line along the line-of-touch, and
    — while throwing in the ball, he must not put any part of either foot in the field-of-play.

    If any of the foregoing is infringed, the opposing team shall have the right, at its option, to throw in the ball or to take a scrummage. If on the second occasion the ball is not thrown in correctly a scrummage shall be formed and the ball shall be put in by the team which threw it in on the first occasion.

### Beginning and End of Line-out

11. The line-out begins when the ball leaves the hands of the player throwing it in.

12. The line-out ends when:

    — a ruck or maul is taking place and all feet of players in the ruck or maul have moved beyond the line-of-touch, or
    — a player carrying the ball leaves the line-out, or

— the ball has been passed, knocked back or kicked from the line-out, or

— the ball is thrown beyond a position fifteen metres from the touch line, or

— the ball becomes unplayable.

**Peeling off**
**'Peeling off' occurs when a player (or players) moves from his position in the line-out for the purpose of catching the ball when it has been passed or knocked back by another of his team in the line-out.**

13.  When the ball is in touch players who approach the line-of-touch must *always* be presumed to do so for the purpose of forming a line-out. Except in a peeling off movement such players must not leave the line-of-touch, or the line-out when formed, until the line-out has ended. A player must not begin to peel off until the ball has left the hands of the player throwing it in.
     **Exception:**
     At a quick throw-in, when a player may come to the line-of-touch and retire from that position without penalty.

14.  In a peeling off movement a player must move parallel and close to the line-out. He must keep moving until a ruck or maul is formed and he joins it or the line-out ends.

**Restrictions on Players in Line-out**
15.  *Before* the ball has been thrown in and has touched the ground or has touched or been touched by a player, players in the line-out must not:
     a.  be off-side, or
     b.  push, charge, shoulder or bind with or in any way hold another player of either team, or
     c.  use any other player as a support to enable him to jump for the ball, or
     d.  stand within five metres of the touch line or prevent the ball from being thrown five metres.

16. *After* the ball has touched the ground or touched or been touched by a player, any player in the line-out must not:
    a. be off-side, or
    b. hold, push shoulder or obstruct an opponent not holding the ball, or
    c. charge an opponent except in an attempt to tackle him or to play the ball.

17. Except when jumping for the ball or peeling off, each player in the line-out must remain at least one metre from the next player of his team until the ball has touched or has been touched by a player or has touched the ground.

It is illegal for a player to lever himself up off another player

18. Except when jumping for the ball or peeling off, a clear space of 500 mm must be left between the two lines of players until the ball has touched or has been touched by a player or has touched the ground.

19. A player in the line-out may move into the space between the touch line and the five metres mark only when the ball has been thrown beyond him and, if he does so, he must not move towards his goal line before the line-out ends, except in a peeling off movement.

20. Until the line-out ends, no player may move beyond a position fifteen metres from the touch line except as allowed when the ball is thrown beyond that position, in accordance with the Exception following Law 24D(1)(d).

**Restrictions on Players not in Line-out**

21. Players of either team who are not in the line-out may not advance from behind the line-out and take the ball from the throw-in except only:

> — a player at a quick throw-in, or
>
> — a player advancing at a long throw-in, or
>
> — a player 'participating in the line-out' (as defined in Section D of Law 24) who may run into a gap in the line-out and take the ball provided he does not charge or obstruct any player in the line-out.

**Penalty:**

a. For an infringement of paragraphs (1), (2), (3), (4), (5), (8), (13), (14), (15)(d), (17), (18) or (19) a free kick fifteen metres from the touch line along the line-of-touch.

b. For an infringement of paragraphs (15)(a) to (c), (16) or (20), a penalty kick fifteen metres from the touch line along the line-of-touch.

c. For an infringement of paragraph (21), a penalty kick on the offending team's off-side line (as defined in Law 24 D) opposite the place of infringement, but not less then fifteen metres from the touch line.

**Place of Scrummage:**
Any scrummage taken or ordered under this Law or as the result of any infringement in a line-out shall be formed fifteen metres from the touch line along the line-of-touch.

# LAW 23

## TOUCH AND LINE-OUT

This is undoubtedly the most contentious area in the game of rugby football, with no fewer than twenty-seven penable offences possible at any one line-out, resulting in either a penalty or free kick! In dealing with the line-out it is necessary to split the subject into a few main headings. As in other topics, a sound knowledge of the law is essential, not just for referees but also players, coaches and spectators.

1. *Ball in Touch*
   The ball is in touch when
   a  The ball is not being carried by a player (eg after it has been kicked) and it touches a touch line or the ground or a person or object on, or beyond it.
      The players should use same ball for the throw-in.
   b. The ball being carried by a player and the player carrying it touches a touch line or the ground beyond it. For referees this is not a time to relax, especially when there is a 'quick throw' (see also Law 6b).

2. *Formation of Line-out*
   There are two kinds of line out:
   a. Normal line-out (orthodox)
   b. Shortened line-out (at discretion of throwing-in side)

   **Normal Line-out** – Prior to commencement.
   The line-out is formed by at least two players from each side lining up in single lines parallel to the line-of-touch.

(The line-of-touch is an imaginary line running infield from where the ball went into touch.)

— the team throwing the ball in determines the number of players in the line-out.
— if the team throwing the ball in-line up less than the normal number, for example seven players, their opponents must be given the opportunity to reduce by retiring from the line-out.
— if players are so retiring and the line-out takes place and ends, then these players can still rejoin play.
— once players have joined the line-out they may not withdraw unless they are from the non-throwing side as detailed above.
— players must be in a straight line, a *slight* latitude is allowed for the jumpers who may be slightly outwith.

The line-out stretches from the five metre line to the fifteen metre line.

— a player who is beyond the fifteen metre line is not in the line-out.

Players in the line-out must observe spacing therein.

— one metre from a player of his own team until the ball is touched or it touches a player.
— half a metre from the opposition until the ball is touched or it touches a player.
— players can face in any direction so long as spaces are observed.

The three-quarters, excluding the scrum half, must be ten metres back from the line-of-touch.

— the three-quarters must remain the ten metres back until the line-out ends or they anticipate a long throw (see beginning of line-out), if they fail to do this it will result in a penalty ten metres back from the line-of-touch and at least fifteen metres from the touch line.

The scrum half remains between the five metre and fifteen metre lines.

— the scrum half can only go beyond the fifteen metre line if he is going for a long throw.

**Short line-out** – Prior to commencement.

As per above only the team throwing in the ball determines the numbers of players (minimum 2) who may participate.

This will ensure less contact and gives the referee a clearer picture of what is liable to occur.

**Beginning of Line-out**
The line-out begins when the ball leaves the hands of the player throwing it in. During the time after the line-out begins until it ends, players must not:

a. leave the line-out unless it is in a peeling-off movement – such a player cannot leave the line-out until it has begun, he must keep moving until the line-out ends or a ruck or maul forms and he joins in.

— referees will watch for the player who leaves the line-out to sweep the ball, if he leaves the line-out while it is still in progress and does not keep moving, he should be penalised (free kick).

— if the peeling player collects the ball correctly and then runs back into his own players in the line-out, it is obstruction (penalty kick at place of infringement).
However, if the referee feels it was unintentional, he will award a scrum for accidental off-side.

— if a peeling movement takes place around the front of the line-out the player who has thrown the ball must not 'take-out' his opposite number to allow the ball carrier a clear run between the five metre line and touch (penalty kick fifteen metres from touch along line-of-touch).

b. be off-side
— this refers to players participating in the line-out and three-quarters (who must be ten metres back from line-of-touch) but three-quarters can advance for a long throw. The three-quarters of the team throwing the ball in must advance first and the ball must be thrown to them, if not, a penalty ten metres back from the line-of-touch and not less than fifteen metres from the touch line will be awarded.
— the player at the tail of the line-out can go beyond the fifteen metre line to win the ball but the ball must be thrown to him (penalty kick fifteen metres from touch along line-of-touch).
— players must stay on their own side of the line-out. If a player who jumps for the ball lands over the off-side line he should be allowed to retire immediately without penalty (penalty kick fifteen metres from touch along line-of-touch).
— the scrum half must stand between the five metre and fifteen metre lines unless going beyond the fifteen metre line for a throw. In this case the ball must reach him, if not, a penalty kick fifteen metres from touch along the line-of-touch will be awarded.

c. Push, charge, shoulder or bind with or hold players of either team (penalty kick fifteen metres from touch along line-of-touch).
— jumpers must not lever themselves off opponents shoulders with their inside arm and jump with their outside arm for ball.

— supporting players, usually props cannot cross
the line-of-touch to protect own jumpers or
obstruct opposite jumpers and their supporting
players.

The difference between legal blocking and illegal
obstruction is exceptionally fine and will be discussed in
detail later.

— referees will watch for supporting players
binding onto their own jumpers before a jumper
touches the ball. This may also lead to the lifting
of a jumper.

Illegal lifting of player in line-out

The thrower's team will know the position to which the ball is being thrown (code) and players will jump or block accordingly.

> — teams cannot close the one metre gaps between themselves or the half metre gap between teams until the ball is touched (free kick fifteen metre from touch along line-of-touch).

The player in front of the jumper is responsible for closing the space immediately behind him. Similarly the player behind the jumper will be responsible for closing the space immediately in front of him.

(Players in front close behind.)

(Players behind close in front.)

> — in a short line-out, the scrum half can enter the line-out to jump for the ball as long as he does not come into contact with opposition players.

If any of the above are infringed a penalty will be awarded to the non-offending side. The exception to this is closing the one metre or half metre gaps, when a free kick on the fifteen metre line will be awarded.

Once the line-out ends, referees should watch for players of the team who have won the ball obstructing or holding back opponents who are trying to get the ball or get to the man who has the ball, and will penalise accordingly.

## Ending of Line-Out

The line-out ends when,

> a. a ruck or maul takes place and the feet of all the players move beyond the line-of-touch.
>> — for a maul to form and a line-out still to be in progress a player must catch the ball cleanly and return to the ground within the confines of the line-out.
>> — similarly for a ruck to form, the ball must be placed on the ground within the confines of the line-out.

b. a player who has caught the ball leaves the line-out.
   — leaving the line-out means the player moves outwith the straight line formed by the rest of his team.

c. the ball is passed, knocked back or kicked from the line-out.
   — if the ball is deflected beyond a shoulder's width from the straight line, the line-out is deemed to be ended.

d. the ball is thrown beyond the fifteen metre line.
   — this becomes open play but the movements of the three-quarters line, scrum half and tail man in the line-out must not be early as described previously.

e. the ball becomes unplayable.
   — a scrummage will be awarded immediately.

## THE SUBTLE DIFFERENCES BETWEEN BLOCKING AND OBSTRUCTING

In discussing the above subject, the following points of law need to be considered.

a. 'Until the ball is thrown in, each player in the line-out must stand at least one metre from the next player of his team in the line-out and avoid physical contact with any other player'.

b. 'A clear space of 500 mm between the shoulders of opposing players, must be left between the two lines of players'.

c. 'The line-out begins when the ball leaves the hands of the player throwing it in'.

d. 'Before the ball has been thrown in and has touched the ground or has touched or been touched by a player, any player must not,
   i.   be off-side, or
   ii.  push, charge, shoulder or bind with or in any way hold another player of either team, or

      iii.  use any other player as a support to enable him to jump for the ball, or

      iv.  stand, within five metres of the touch line or prevent the ball from being thrown five metres'.

  e. 'After the ball has touched the ground or touched or been touched by a player, any player in the line-out must not,

      i.  be off-side, or

      ii.  hold, push, shoulder or obstruct an opponent not holding the ball, or

      iii.  charge an opponent except in an attempt to tackle him or play the ball'.

  f. 'Except when jumping for the ball or peeling off, each player in the line-out must remain at least one metre from the next player of his team until the ball has touched or been touched by a player or has touched the ground'.

  g. 'Except when jumping for the ball or peeling off, a clear space of 500 mm must be left between the two lines of players until the ball has touched or has been touched by a player or has touched the ground'.

You will immediately observe from the above sections of Law 23 that they all demand consideration, at least in part, in any attempt to determine the differences between blocking and obstructing.

First of all, let us attempt to clarify what is meant by 'blocking' and 'obstruction'.

Considering 'obstruction' first, the law makers require referees to take a firm hand against this illegal practice, whether it be in the line-out or for that matter, any other phase of the game.

We have heard many times that the philosophy in framing the laws, has been to reward good play and punish bad play.

Wilful forms of obstruction such as jumping off the shoulders of an opponent, charging of players in the opposition line-out, holding players not in possession of the ball, premature binding on their own or opposition players, in fact, all forms of wilful interference are illegal and should be punished subject to the advantage law, by the awarding of a penalty fifften metres in from the touch line along the line-of-touch.

Whether advantage should be played from the above mentioned situations is for the referee to decide. However, in doing so, he should give serious consideration to the possibility of foul play occurring (retaliation), which is often a result of the referee not taking strong and decisive action immediately in these situations.

Blocking on the other hand should be considered in an entirely different light.

For example, let us consider the situation of players legally binding on the 'catcher', who has possession of the ball in the line-out.

Clearly, when the ball is subsequently delivered to the scrum half, all the forwards in front of him are technically off-side and very often 'legally' provide him with protection, or if you like, temporarily obstruct the opposition forwards from getting at him.

In this instance, whilst obstruction has taken place, it would be quite wrong of the referee to penalise since the laws provide for players to bind on each other to form either a maul or a ruck once the ball has been played.

The above example is common in any game and is typical of what players and coaches describe as 'blocking' or 'legal obstruction'.

The laws are quite clear in stating what players in the line-out can and cannot do before the ball has touched or has been touched by a player or has touched the ground.

Put simply, this means that all support players must not move until the catcher has touched the ball or if they themselves are jumping for the ball.

However, the International Rugby Football Board has philosophised on many occasions that the laws of the game are written to protect and reward players with skill. At the same time, they have shown great concern for the safety of players participating in the game.

Picture the situation, therefore, of a player decisively out-jumping his opponent, only to have his legs cut from under him at the top of his jump. Clearly dangerous play!

It is for this reason that many referees allow early movement towards the jumper, to enable support of him at the top of his jump. They will not allow blatant 'lifting' (penalty) but provided

*Courtesy of The Scotsman*

LEGAL BINDING IN THE LINE OUT:- The ball has been won and the team with the hooped jerseys are legally binding on their own team mate so protecting the ball. Law 23.

the jumper can get off the ground unaided they will allow early movement, thereby rewarding skill and ensuring player safety.

This is a good example of 'practical' refereeing. Players appreciate a referee who rewards skill. In addition, a good line-out jumper likes to know he can demonstrate that skill, without the risk of being interfered with in his attempt to secure the ball.

Early movement allowed by the referee means that the catcher, having jumped unaided, is protected from possible subsequent foul play, which may result in injury. As a consequence of understanding the philosophy in framing the law, the referee has applied the spirit of the law, if not exactly applying the letter of the law. Remember: sometimes the best law of all is Law 29 – common sense!

ILLEGAL LIFTING IN THE LINE OUT:- Law 23.

Naturally, if a line-out ends with tapped ball, members of the team winning the ball will obstruct players from the opposition from getting at the scrum half, slmply by their physical presence. This situation is not 'illegal' obstruction in itself and should not be penalised.

If, however, an opposition player in attempting to come through the line-out is charged or held and is thus prevented from getting at the ball, this is clearly obstruction and should be penalised.

A well organised team will always make it difficult (quite legally) for their opponents to get at the ball or the scrum half in possession of the ball after a line-out has ended.

Referees should penalise blatant forms of obstruction, but should allow play to proceed if legal blocking occurs.

In summary, in determining the subtle differences between blocking and obstruction, the referee should consider the following:

- a. The intent of the offending player(s).
- b. Whether either team has gained an unfair advantage as a result of their actions.
- c. The safety of the players involved.

Of course, in considering refereeing of the line-out in the broader sense, a preventative refereeing approach will minimise the likelihood of obstruction.

The following general principles are therefore recommended to referees:

- a. Insist on proper spacings, right throughout the entire game. This will make it difficult for many forms of obstruction to take place. If obstruction then occurs, you will find it easier to detect.
- b. Let players know that charging, holding, jumping off shoulders etc will not be tolerated. Penalise immediately if infringements occur.

c. Do not watch the ball, but rather closely observe players in the vicinity of where the ball is being thrown.

d. Be consistent. Your approach to the last line-out of the game should be the same as for the first.

## CONTROL IN THE LINE-OUT FOR REFEREES TO THE BENEFIT OF PLAYERS AND COACHES

Total control in the line-out is impossible to achieve because of the number of offences in any one line-out, a total twenty-seven. A line-out of course can stretch from the five metres to fifteen metres line or beyond which again makes it difficult for the referee to control.

- What does control mean?
- Strictly administering the letter of the law?
- Assuring mayhem doesn't ensue?
- Assuring fair play is observed?
- Making sure the best line-out wins the ball?
- Allowing constructive play and discouraging destructive play?

Every referee has his own ideas on the question, and his own answers. They depend on his attitude to the game, the standard of the game, the players attitude to the game, any competitive influences on the game and many more. Possibly the answer lies in a little of all of the above plus the most important factor – common sense.

The following points are some phases of the line-out that a referee will consider when assessing his own method of controlling the line-out.

1. *Formation of the line-out*
   It is desirable for the referee to arrive at the position for the line-out as early as possible. From here, the referee can watch the players taking up their positions. He can immediately determine when the line-out has been formed ie two from each side in the line-out. He can be

aware of any potential problem by observing the players attitudes and any ill feeling as they form the line-out.

As the line-out forms, he can ensure that the required gaps between players are given. This is probably the most important point in assuring fair play in the line-out as it is very difficult to infringe the laws unobserved with wide open gaps. Clear gaps allow the referee to see more easily all that goes on.

2. *Position of the jumpers*
   The referee should always be aware of who the key jumpers are for each team. Obviously play will be centred near these players and this is where attention is required before, as, and after the ball is thrown in.

3. *Protection of the jumpers*
   A line-out jumper is very vulnerable at the top of his leap. The laws do not allow him to be helped but do allow for support after he has caught the ball. It is very important to make sure he is not interfered with before the throw and most importantly, when he is in the air. Action such as the opposition tipping the jumper is highly dangerous and will be penalised.

4. *Destructive Tactics*
   These are mostly employed by the non-throwing in team or the weaker line-out team. The most common tactics are:
   a. Barging. This can be by an individual and it usually occurs on the jumper before the throw in. If it is done professionally, only just before the catch, it is more difficult to observe. Also a team can barge in unison. The most common method is that of the whole line-out bunches up and takes a step across the line-of-touch, as one. The aim is to bump all the opponents out and thus make the line-out a non contest.
   b. Jumping off the shoulder. Most people feel that this

should be easy to detect, however, some players are
very adept at it. Referees are suspicious of the player
who taps the ball using his outside arm. Where is his
other arm? The most inflammatory method is to jump
off the opposition but he may also close the gaps and
jump off his own players.

c. Holding an opponent. This can involve very subtle
   holding of the opposition jumper which just puts him
   off balance and is very irritating to the jumper. Also of
   equal import is the player who holds his opponent in
   order to stop line chasing after the ball. This is usually

Illegal barging in line-out

at the back of the line-out and regularly causes an
altercation.

5. *Jumping across the line-of-touch and off-side*
Often unsuccessful jumpers end on the opponents side.
Referees will make sure they do not interfere with play
and retire to their own side as soon as possible. Also it is
important to differentiate between the genuine jumper
and the player who moves into an off-side position in
order to obstruct or get a start and who claims he is
jumping.

Illegal obstruction of player in the line-out

6. *Verbal Intimidation*

   This is as much contrary to the law and as likely to cause a flare up as any of the preceding points. Referees will not allow this unnecessary niggling talk.

7. *Position of the Referee*

   The position taken for every line-out varies depending on the dictates of that line-out. However, if we are only considering control, the following are the most important factors for a good referee.

   a. Regularly be at the front so you can be seen as a deterrent.
   b. When you have identified the trouble spot, be near that point.
   c. Tend to stand closer to players than normal.
   d. Be mobile so players cannot predict where you will be.
   e. Watch for an intentional knock-on by the attacking side. This can be difficult to detect and close to the line presents try-scoring opportunities.

   The line-out is often referred to 'as the illegitimiate child of Rugby Union'. Apart from the number of players it is the major difference between Rugby Union and Rugby League, and with twenty-seven offences in any one line-out, it is the most difficult aspect of the game to referee.

# LAW 24
## *Off-Side*

Off-side means that a player is in a position in which he is out of the game and is liable to penalty.

In general play the player is in an off-side position because he is in front of the ball when it has been last played by another player of his team.

In play at scrummage, ruck, maul or line-out the player is off-side because he remains or advances in front of the line or place stated in, or otherwise infringes, the relevant sections of this Law.

### A. OFF-SIDE IN GENERAL PLAY

1 A player is in an off-side position if the ball has been:
— kicked, or
— touched, or
— is being carried
by one of his team behind him.

2. There is no penalty for being in an off-side position unless:
   a. the player plays the ball or obstructs an opponent, or
   b. he approaches or remains within ten metres of an opponent waiting to play the ball or the place where the ball pitches. Where no opponent is waiting to play the ball but one arrives as the ball pitches, a player in an off-side position must not obstruct or interfere with him.

### Exceptions
   i. When an off-side player cannot avoid being touched by the ball or by a player carrying it, he is 'accidentally off-side'. Play should be allowed to continue unless the infringing team obtains an advantage, in which case a scrummage shall be formed at that place.
   ii. A player who receives an unintentional throw-forward is not off-side.
   iii. If, because of the speed of the game, an offside player finds himself unavoidably within ten metres of an opponent waiting to play the ball or the place where the

ball pitches, he shall not be penalised provided he retires without delay and without interfering with the opponent.

**Penalty**

Penalty kick at the place of infringement, or, at the option of the non-offending team, a scrummage at the place where the ball was last played by the offending team. If the latter place is in In-goal, the penalty kick shall be taken or the scrummage shall be formed five metres from the goal line, on a line through the place.

## B.   OFF-SIDE AT SCRUMMAGE

**The term 'off-side line' means a line parrallel to the goal lines through the hindmost foot of the player's team in the scrummage.**

While a scrummage is forming or is taking place:

1. A player is off-side if:
   a. he joins it from his opponents' side, or
   b. he, not being in the scrummage nor the player of either team who puts the ball in the scrummage,
      — fails to retire behind the off-side line or to his goal line whichever is the nearer, or
      — places either foot in front of the off-side line while the ball is in the scrummage.

A player may leave a scrummage provided he retires immediately behind the off-side line.

If he wishes to rejoin the scrummage, he must do so behind the ball.

He may not play the ball as it emerges between the feet of his front row if he is in front of the off-side line.

**Exception**

The restrictions on leaving the scrummage in front of the off-side line do not apply to a player taking part in 'wheeling' a scrummage providing he immediately plays the ball.

2. A player is off-side if he, being the player of either team who puts the ball in the scrummage, remains or places either foot in front of the ball while it is in the scrummage.

3. A player is off-side if he, being the immediate opponent of the player putting in the ball, takes up a position on or moves to the opposite side of the scrummage in front of the off-side line.

**Penalty**
Penalty kick at the place of infringement.

## C.   OFF-SIDE AT RUCK OR MAUL
**The term 'off-side line' means a line parrallel to the goal lines through the hindmost foot of the player's team in the ruck or maul.**

1. **Ruck or Maul otherwise than at Line-out**
   While a ruck or maul is taking place (including a ruck or maul which continues after a line-out has ended) a player is off-side if he:-
   a. joins it from his opponent' side, or
   b. joins it in front of the ball, or
   c. does not join the ruck or maul but fails to retire behind the off-side line *without delay* or
   d. unbinds from the ruck or leaves the maul and does not *immediately* either rejoin it behind the ball or retire behind the off-side, or
   e. advances beyond the off-side line with either foot and does not join the ruck or maul

**Penalty**
Penalty kick at the place of infringement.

2. **Ruck or Maul at Line-out**
   The term 'participating in the line-out' has the same meaning as in Section D of this Law. A player participating in the line-out is not obliged to join or remain in the ruck or maul and if he is not in the ruck or maul he continues to participate in the line-out until it has ended.

While a line-out is in progress and a ruck or maul takes place, a player is off-side if he:-

a. joins the ruck or maul from his opponent's side, or

b. joins it in front of the ball, or

c. being a player who is participating in the line-out and is not in the ruck or maul, does not retire to and remain at the off-side line defined in this Section.

**Penalty**

Penalty kick fifteen metres from the touch-line along the line-of-touch.

d. being a player who is not participating in the line-out, remains or advances with either foot in front of the off-side line defined in Section of this Law.

**Penalty**

Penalty kick on the offending team's off-side line opposite the place of infringement, but not less than fifteen metres from the touch line.

## D.    OFF-SIDE AT LINE-OUT

**The term 'participating in the line-out' refers exclusively to the following players:-**

- those players who are in the line-out, and
- the player who throws in the ball, and
- his immediate opponent who may have the option of throwing in the ball, and
- one other player of either team who takes up position to receive the ball if it is passed or knocked back from the line-out.

All other players are *not* participating in the line-out.

The term 'off-side line' means a line ten metres behind the line-of-touch and parallel to the goal lines or, if the goal line be nearer than ten metres to the line-of-touch, the 'off-side line' is the goal line.

### Off-side while participating in line-out

1. A participating player is off-side if:-

a. *before* the ball has touched a player or the ground he wilfully remains or advances with either foot in front of the line-of-touch, unless he advances solely in the act of jumping for the ball, or

b. *after* the ball has touched a player or the ground, if he is not carrying the ball, he advances with either foot in front of the ball, unless he is lawfully tackling or attempting to tackle an opponent who is participating in the line-out. Such tackle or attempt to tackle must, however, start from his side of the ball, or

c. in a peeling off movement he fails to keep moving close to the line-out until a ruck or maul is formed and he joins it or the line-out ends, or

d. before the line-out ends he moves beyond a position fifteen metres from the touch line.

**Exception**
Players of the team throwing in the ball move beyond a position fifteen metres from the touch line for a long throw-in to them. They may do so only when the ball leaves the hands of the player throwing it in and if they do so their opponents participating in the line-out may follow them. If players so move and the ball is not thrown in to or beyond them they must be penalised for off-side.

**Penalty**
Penalty kick fifteen metres from the touch line along the line of touch.

2. The player throwing in the ball and his immediate opponent must:-
   a. remain within five metres of the touch line, or
   b. retire to the off-side line, or
   c. join the line-out after the ball has been thrown in five metres, or
   d. move into position to receive the ball if it is passed or knocked back from the line-out provided no other player is occupying that position at that line-out.

### Off-side while not participating in line-out

3. A player who is not participating is off-side if before the line-out has ended he advances or remains with either foot in front of the off-side line.

### Exception

Players of the team throwing in the ball who are not participating in the line-out may advance for a long throw-in to them beyond the line-out. They may do so only when the ball leaves the hands of the player throwing in the ball and, if they do their opponents may advance to meet them. If players so advance for a long throwin to them and the ball is not thrown to them they must be penalised for off-side.

### Players returning to 'on-side' position

4. A player is not obliged, before throwing in the ball, to wait until players of his team have returned to or behind the line-out but such players are off-side unless they return to an on-side position *without delay*.

### Penalty

Penalty kick on the offending team's off-side line (as defined in Section D of this Law) opposite the place of infringement but not less than fifteen metres from the touch line.

## LAW 24

### Off-side in general play

Most off-sides in this aspect of the game come about when a player is in an off-side position when the ball has been kicked by one of his team behind him in a kick ahead or 'up and under' situation.

The referee should whistle at once if an off-side player, who cannot be placed on-side, charges within ten metres of an opponent waiting to receive the ball. Delay may prove dangerous to the catcher. The off-side player can only move within ten metres of the catcher when either the kicker or a player of the same team behind the kicker has moved forward following the kick and passed him. Where there is no opponent waiting to field the kick ahead but one arrives as the ball pitches, an off-side player who is near to that player must not obstruct or interfere with him in any way whatsoever before he is put on-side.

If a player kicks the ball which is mis fielded by an opponent and the ball is then played by another player of the kicker's team in an off-side position within ten metres of the opponent, a penalty kick should be awarded or a scrum back at the point of kick at the option of the non-offending team.

However, a penalty for off-side should not be given at once if the non-offending team gains an advantage or if it appears likely to gain an advantage; but if the expected advantage is not gained, the penalty should in all cases be awarded even if it is necessary to bring play back for that purpose to the place of infringement. The point where the ball pitches also applies when the ball has struck a goal-post or crossbar. Off-side players must not approach or remain within ten metres of the defender waiting to catch the rebound.

If an attacking player kicks the ball which is charged down by an opponent and another attacking player within ten metres of the opponent then plays the ball, play should be allowed to continue as the opponent was not 'waiting to play the ball'.

When a player knocks on and an off-side player of the same team next plays the ball, a penalty for off-side will not be awarded unless the off-side deprives the non-offending team of an advantage, for example, nearest non-offending opponent thirty metres away – a scrum; three metres away – a penalty. If this situation arises In-goal then a penalty try could be awarded.

There are obviously exceptions, because of the speed of the game, when an off-side player cannot avoid being touched by the ball or by a player carrying it. In these cases he is deemed to be 'accidentally off-side' and play will be allowed to continue, unless the infringing team obtains an unfair advantage, in which case a scrummage will be awarded.

## Off-side at a Scrum

The scrum and its various penalties have been covered earlier, but remember all non-participants of a scrum must retire without delay to the scrummage off-side line when a scrummage is forming. Loiterers must be penalised. Once the ball has been won check non-ball-winning wing forwards breaking off retire to the 'hind most foot line' – usually that of the number 8's feet and the same team's backs are also not in front of that line even if the referee has to swing round a few times because of the position of the scrum, to check on them.

Any player of either team may at a particular scrum be the scrum half, but for that particular scrum he is the only player who does not have to adhere to the hindmost foot law; so long as he stays on the side of the scrum the ball was put into.

## Off-side Ruck or Maul

Off-side at the ruck or maul has already been covered in Laws 21 and 22. Basically, everyone not in either a ruck or maul must stay behind the hindmost foot including the scrum half. As these are maybe second or third phase possession plays referees must be especially watchful for the backs of the side not winning the ball creeping up to and beyond the off-side line of the hindmost foot of the ruck or maul.

## Off-side at Line-out

The various offences have been covered earlier. The off-side penalty offence which occurs most at a line-out concerns the backs and not being ten metres back from the line-of-touch. Remember players who advance beyond the off-side line or who move beyond a position fifteen metres from the touch line in the expectation of a long throw-in must be penalised if, for any reason (including the hooker not having the strength to reach them) the ball is not thrown beyond that position. If a player not participating in the line-out is off-side, the referee should not whistle immediately if the opposing team is likely to gain an advantage.

Nowadays it is usually the hooker who throws the ball in from touch, if so, remember the wing three-quarter nearest the line-out must retire to the off-side line along with the rest of the backs.

At all times the referee should be strict in dealing with those players who, while not disputing possession of the ball in the line-out, advance to an off-side position whether intentionally or not. However, a player jumping unsuccessfully for the ball who crosses the line-of-touch should be given an opportunity to retire before being penalised.

Off-side at a line-out is covered in greater detail in Law 23 but remember the good referee will always apply the advantage law at any off-side decision not just at the line-out but also at a scrum, ruck or maul and in general play.

# LAW 25
## *On-Side*

On-side means that a player is in the Game and not liable to penalty for off-side.

### Player made on-side by action of his team

1. Any player who is off-side in general play, *including* an off-side player who is within ten metres of an opponent waiting to play the ball or the place where the ball pitches and is retiring as required, becomes on-side as a result of any of the following actions of his team:

> — when the off-side player has retired behind the player of his team who last kicked, touched or carried the ball, or
> — when one of his team carrying the ball has run in front of him, or
> — when one of his team has run in front of him after coming from the place or from behind the place where the ball was kicked.

In order to put the off-side player on-side, this other player must be in the playing area, but he is not debarred from following up in touch or touch-in-goal.

### Player made on-side by action of opposing team

2. Any player who is off-side in general play, *except* an off-side player within ten metres of an opponent waiting to play the ball or the place where the ball pitches, becomes on-side as a result of any of the following actions:

> — when an opponent carrying the ball has run five metres, or
> — when an opponent kicks or passes the ball, or
> — when an opponent *intentionally* touches the ball and does not catch or gather it.

An off-side player within ten metres of an opponent waiting to play the ball or the place where the ball pitches *cannot* be put on-side by *any* action of his opponents.

Any *other* off-side player in general play is *always* put on-side when an opponent plays the ball.

**Player retiring at scrummage, ruck, maul or line-out**

3. A player who is in an off-side position when a scrummage, ruck, maul or line-out is forming or taking place and is retiring as required by Law 24(Off-side) becomes on-side:

— when an opponent carrying the ball has run five metres, or

— when an opponent has kicked the ball.

An off-side player in this situation is *not* put on-side when an opponent passes the ball.

# LAW 25

The important point here which many people forget is that an off-side player (except in general play) is not put on-side when opponents merely catch and pass the ball on from player to player. Hence, when a team has gained quick possession from a scrummage, ruck, maul or line-out and starts a passing movement, opponents who are retiring must not be allowed to interfere in the movement unless an opponent runs five metres with the ball or an opponent kicks the ball.

An off-side player who is within ten metres of an opponent waiting to play the ball or the place where the ball pitches must retire and continue to do so up to ten metres until he is put on-side. The referee should be careful to ensure that no benefit is gained by loiterers who wilfully remain in an off-side position and thereby prevent opponents from running with, kicking, passing or otherwise playing the ball. If a player wilfully remains in an off-side position must be penalised after the referee has allowed the possibility of advantage.

# LAW 26
## *Foul Play*

Foul Play is any action by a player which is contrary to the letter and spirit of the Game and includes obstruction, unfair play, misconduct, dangerous play, unsporting behaviour, retaliation and repeated infringements.

## Obstruction
1. It is illegal for any player:
    a. who is running for the ball to charge or push an opponent also running for the ball, except shoulder to shoulder,
    b. who is in an off-side position wilfully to run or stand in front of another player of his team who is carrying the ball, thereby preventing an opponent from reaching the latter player,
    c. who is carrying the ball after it has come out of a scrummage, ruck, maul or line-out, to attempt to force his way through the players of his team in front of him,
    d. who is an outside player in a scrummage or ruck to prevent an opponent from advancing round the scrummage or ruck.

## Unfair Play, Repeated Infringements
2. It is illegal for any player:
    a. deliberately to play unfairly or wilfully infringe any Law of the Game,
    b. wilfully to waste time,
    c. wilfully to knock or throw the ball from the playing area into touch, touch-in-goal or over the dead-ball line,
    d. to infringe repeatedly any Law of the Game.

## Misconduct, Dangerous Play
3. It is illegal for any player:
    a. to strike an opponent,
    b. wilfully to hack or kick an opponent or to trip him with the foot or to trample on an opponent lying on the ground,
    c. to tackle early, or late or dangerously, including the action known as 'a stiff arm tackle',
    d. who is not running for the ball wilfully to charge or obstruct an opponent who has just kicked the ball,

e. to hold, push, charge, obstruct or grasp an opponent not holding the ball except in a scrummage, ruck or maul.
(*Except in a scrummage or ruck the dragging away of a player lying close to the ball is permitted. Otherwise pulling any part of the clothing of an opponent is holding.*)

f. in the front row of a scrummage to form down some distance from the opponents and rush against them,

g. wilfully to cause a scrummage, ruck or maul to collapse,

h. while the ball is out of play to molest, obstruct or in any way interfere with an opponent or be guilty of any form of misconduct,

i. to commit any misconduct on the playing area which is prejudicial to the spirit of good sportsmanship.

**Player Ordered Off**

A player who is ordered off shall take no futher part in the match. When a player is ordered off, the referee shall, as soon as possible after the match, send to the Union or other disciplinary body having

*Courtesy of The Scotsman*

DANGEROUS HIGH TACKLE:- Part Law 26 (3) on dangerous play.

jurisdiction over the match a report naming the player and describing the circumstances which necessitated the ordering off. The Union or other disciplinary body having jurisdiction over the match, shall consider such report and any other evidence they deem appropriate. They shall then take such action and impose such punishment as they see fit.

# LAW 26

The law on foul play is divided into three clear sections.

## 1. Obstruction

It is not possible for a player carrying the ball to be penalised for obstruction. If a player is guilty of obstruction, the referee is required by the International Board to caution or order off the guilty player, depending on the severity of the obstruction.

Types of obstruction are many and varied ranging from players being taken out of the game by early tackles while attempting to secure the ball, to preventing opposition players from tackling the ball carrier.

If opposition players are running for the ball they are allowed to push each other as long as it is shoulder to shoulder ie a shoulder charge. A player who runs into another and hits him with his shoulder on any other part of his opponent's body other than the shoulder should be penalised for foul play.

Section 1(b) would, amongst other things, cover the situation where a three-quarter runs in front of a fellow three-quarter with the ball and so prevents an opposition player tackling the ball carrier. It would also cover the situation, similar to American football, where a player runs in front of the ball carrier taking opposition players out and so preventing a tackle on the ball carrier.

Although it is not very often penalised, a ball carrier is not allowed to force his way through his own side in front of him who are taking part in scrums, rucks, mauls and particularly lines-out. This often happens in a line-out where the sweeper on receiving the ball runs into his own players in front of him in an attempt to set up a maul or second phase ball.

At scrums referees should be aware of a wing forward swinging his body out when the ball is in the scrummage in an attempt to prevent the opposition scrum half from moving round the scrum. If the wing forward binds at an angle before the scrum starts that is acceptable, but once the scrum has commenced, he is not able to swing his body outwards.

The penalty for the infringements in section 1 of the law is a penalty at the place of infringement or a penalty try if a try would probably have been scored.

### 2. Unfair Play & Repeated Infringements

This is the section of the law where the referee has to decide whether or not the first three sub-sections are infringed deliberately. If the referee is unsure about the deliberate nature of the infringement, he should give the benefit of the doubt to the player and not award a penalty kick. If on the other hand, the referee deems the actions of a player to be deliberate, then a penalty kick should be awarded.

Section 2(d) covers *all* aspects of the game. The most common infringement which is penalised in this area is the crooked feed by a scrum half but could be for, amongst other things, persistent killing of the ball at the tackle situation by a wing forward, or a hooker not throwing the ball in straight at a line-out. The referee will usually allow three penalties or free kicks, depending on the nature of the infringement, to be awarded against the offending player before cautioning him. The referee should also have a word with the offending player's captain in an effort to remedy the situation. If the player then repeats the offence he must be ordered off. It should be noted that repeated infringement is a question of fact and not a question of whether the offender intended to offend. Having said that, at lower level or junior games, referees should be more tolerant of repeated infringements due to the possible lack of ability of the players.

The award for infringement of this section of the law is a penalty at the place of infringement. Note that if a player wilfully throws the ball into touch the award is at the place from which the ball was thrown, not fifteen metres in from touch as some people think. If a defending player deliberately throws or knocks the ball into touch-in-goal or over the dead-ball line while he is In-goal, the penalty shall be governed by Law 14. That is, a penalty kick shall be awarded to the attacking side in the field-of-play five metres from the goal line opposite the place of infringement but not within five metres of the touch line. As with other parts of Law 26 a penalty try could be awarded.

### 3.  Misconduct & Dangerous Play

Most players are ordered off by their infringement of this section of the law. Referees are under instruction to ensure that players who offend under this section of the law are at least cautioned and thereafter, if they infringe any section of the law, ordered off. It should be noted that a player does not have to be officially cautioned before he is ordered off but if a player is cautioned, the referee has no option but to order that player off next time he commits a similar offence. Although referees are advised against issuing general warnings, these sometimes have to be administered because of the nature of the game. If a general warning is issued to the captains of both teams, they should then inform their players. Thereafter, if any player infringes Law 26 he has to be ordered off no matter his involvement in the game prior to the general warning.

Referees have been advised that playing the man without the ball, early or late tackles, straight arm tackles and high tackles *must* be penalised. It is for the referee to decide what constitutes a dangerous tackle.  A lot will depend on the apparent intentions of the tackler or the nature of the tackle. It might be that a player is wrong footed by the ball carrier and high tackles him accidentally. A good referee will certainly penalise the high tackle but will appreciate there was no malice and a quick word to the offender rather than an official warning will suffice.

Other aspects which constitute dangerous play are charging the ball carrier while making no attempt to tackle him and if a player taps or pulls the feet of another player who is jumping for the ball. It is now accepted that if a player is off his feet and jumping for the ball either in a line-out or in open play an opponent is not allowed to tackle him until he returns to the ground.

Hitting, kicking or hacking an opponent is to be deplored and referees should be strict in ordering off such players who offend in such a manner. Referees do have problems when a mass punch erupts during a match. Every referee has his own methods of restoring normality to the game, but if the instigator/s can be identified an example should be made of him/them and they should be ordered off. It might be that in this situation a general warning will have to be issued to the captains.

Advantage of course can be played from nearly every instance of foul play apart from collapsed scrums and when it would be dangerous to allow play to continue. Other aspects which the referee would have to consider if he were to allow advantage would be the nature of the offence, the tenure of the game, position on the field and time in the game.

Penalties for misconduct and foul play are clear. A penalty kick, if advantage was not played, or a penalty try if but for the foul play a try would have been scored, would be the awards. Even if advantage is played a caution, either official or a quiet word, or an ordering off should be administered by the referee.

Apart from sections 3(d) and (h), for all incidents of foul play which happen in the field, the penalty kick shall be at the place of infringement. If the penalty is for a 'late tackle' after a player has kicked the ball, ie section 3(d) of the law, the non-offending team shall have the option of the penalty where the ball was kicked from or where the ball first alights. If the ball alights in touch the alternative kick shall be on the fifteen metre line opposite the place where the ball went into touch. If the ball alights within fifteen metres of the touch line again the optional penalty is on the fifteen metres line opposite the place where the ball first bounced. When the ball first bounces either in In-goal or goes into touch-in-goal or over the dead-ball line, the optional penalty in this case should be awarded five metres from the goal line on a line parallel to the touch line through the line where the ball first crossed the goal line. If the position of the resultant penalty is within the fifteen metres line, the kick should be moved out to the fifteen line. For infringements which happen In-goal reference should be made to Law 14.

For section 3(h) of this law, infringements which happen when the ball is out of play, the penalty kick shall be awarded where the ball would next come into play. For example at a line-out the penalty would be on the fifteen metre line of the line-of-touch; within In-goal, either on the twenty-two metre line or five metres from the goal line depending on whether the offence was against the attacking or defending team and after a try was scored, the penalty would be awarded at the centre of the half-way line.

Reference should be made to the position of a penalty kick which is awarded after an offence is reported by a touch judge. A ruling given by the International Rugby Football Board indicated that, in this case, the penalty should be awarded at the place of infringement or else at the place where play would commence. Assuming the referee did not see the offence nor his touch judge flagging, play would continue until the referee's attention was drawn to his touch judge. After consultation and assuming the referee decided to award a penalty, he would award the kick at the most advantageous position to the non-offending team either at the place of infringement or at the place where play would have restarted, even if that place was forty or fifty metres further down the pitch.

## Player Ordered Off

Any player who is ordered off must be reported to the appropriate rugby authorities by the referee. Even if the referee realises afterwards that he has ordered the wrong player off, he must still report the matter to the appropriate body explaining the circumstances. The Union or disciplinary body investigating the case can now, in addition to the referee's written report, call on any other evidence which they deem appropriate, which could be video recordings of the match.

# LAW 27
## *Penalty Kick*

A penalty kick is a kick awarded to the non-offending team as stated in the Laws.

It may be taken by any player of the non-offending team and by any form of kick provided that the kicker, if holding the ball, must propel it out of his hands or, if the ball is on the ground, he must propel it a visible distance from the mark. He may keep his hand on the ball while kicking it.

1.  The non-offending team has the option of taking a scrummage at the mark and shall put in the ball.

2.  When a penalty kick is taken the following shall apply:
    a.  The kick must be taken without undue delay.
    b.  The kick must be taken at or behind the mark on a line through the mark and the kicker may place the ball for a place kick. If the place prescribed by the Laws for the award of a penalty kick is within five metres of the opponent's goal line, the mark for the penalty kick or a scrummage taken instead of it shall be five metres from the goal line on a line through that place.
    c.  The kicker may kick the ball in any direction and he may play the ball again, without any restriction, except that if he has indicated to the referee that he intends to attempt a kick at goal or has taken any action indicating such intention he must not kick the ball in any other way. A player kicking for touch may only punt or drop kick the ball. Any indication of intention is irrevocable.
    d.  The *kicker's team* except the placer for a place kick must be behind the ball until it has been kicked.
    e.  The *opposing team* must run without delay (and continue to do so while the kick is being taken and while the ball is being played by the kicker's team) to or behind a line parallel to the goal lines and ten metres from the mark, or to their own goal line if nearer to the mark. If a kick at goal is taken they must there remain motionless with their hands by their sides until the kick has been taken.

Retiring players will not be penalised if their failure to retire ten metres is due to the rapidity with which the kick has been taken, but they may not stop retiring and enter the game until an opponent carrying the ball has run five metres.

f. The *opposing team* must not prevent the kick or interfere with the kicker in any way. This applies to actions such as wilfully carrying, throwing or kicking the ball away out of reach of the kicker.

**Penalty**

— For an infringement by the kicker's team – a scrummage at the mark.

— For an infringement by the opposing team – a penalty kick ten metres in front of the mark or five metres from the goal line whichever is the nearer on a line through the mark. Any player of the non-offending team may take the kick.

# LAW 27

The penalty kick must always be taken with the ball which was in play unless the referee decides that the ball is defective. This avoids the situation where a player kicking for goal changes to his favourite ball. As stated previously if a kicker takes too long in taking his kick say, because one of his team mates is being treated for injury, the kick should be disallowed and a scrummage ordered with the side who was penalised in the first place putting in. A period of one minute between the indication of intention to kick at goal and the actual kick is well inside the zone of 'undue delay' and any time over forty seconds will be added on.

A player taking a tap penalty must not bounce the ball on his knee. The kick must be made with the foot or lower leg. If the player does not comply with this then the referee should award a scrum.

If, from a penalty kick taken in In-goal, the ball travels into touch-in-goal or over the dead-ball line, a five metres scrummage should be ordered, with the attacking team putting the ball into the scrum.

If the offending team do not retire ten metres and interfere with the non-offending players taking a quick tap penalty and no advantage to the non-offending team accrues, the mark of the penalty will be advanced ten metres. However, remember that no penalty can be taken by the attacking team nearer than five metres to the defending goal line.

### Suggested positions at penalties for referees
*When the kicker is not kicking for goal*
Having indicated the mark, move to the side. Which side you move to should depend, on most occasions, on the distance of the mark from touch. This is because you will wish to see not only the kicker but also those of his side who will be following up. If the mark is near touch, most of the kicker's side will be infield from him and therefore your best position will be on or near the touch line. If the mark is well away from touch, most of the kicker's side is likely to be on the touch line side of him and so your best position will be in-field of the mark.

From a point level with the mark, you will be able to see if the kicker kicks from it, if his players are on-side when he kicks (remember the quick glance behind) and if the opposition have retired to your satisfaction. The distance you should be from the mark is impossible to define, but somewhere between five and ten metres is usually suitable.

One good reason for being well away from the mark is the possibility of the kicker taking a short kick to himself and then running forward and away from touch to widen the angle before kicking or taking a short kick and then passing to a better positioned team-mate.

The short penalty involving some planned and often complicated move is something you must always be prepared for. This may be 'telegraphed', or it may not be. The good referee will anticipate the short penalty and will make sure that he is not in the way of any play, and that he is in a good position to judge the legality of what happens next. He will be aware of the possibility of (a) a tap and pass to a team-mate, followed by almost anything, or, (b) a pivot move. He will be on the look-out for players on dummy runs and will wish to make sure that no player protects the ball carrier by obstruction.

There is no one position from which everything can be seen, but you won't be far wrong if you are level or slightly behind the spot, at which the kick is being taken, and well to the side.

If you can see which way the first pass is likely to go, for example if a pivot move is set up, the best place for you is probably level with the kicker on the opposite side from the pivot. From here you can see most of what goes on and you are unlikely to get in the way of any fancy move, particularly if you hold your ground until you see how play is developing. Resist the temptation to follow the ball immediately after the tap and pass.

*When the kicker is kicking for goal*
You should be in position such that you can see if a player of the kicking side is off-side and if any opposing player has not retired or is not standing still as required. You will want to move so that you are near the posts as soon as possible after the ball has been kicked. At the same time, it is bad practice to run in front of the kicker as he is about to kick.

Therefore, on most occasions you should be approximately level with the kicker as he kicks, ideally on the touch line side, with the ball and kicker between yourself and his following up forwards.

However, if the mark is near a touch line a position even nearer touch may put you too far from the post or developing play. In this case, a position level with the kicker but in-field between him and the rest of his team, is a most acceptable alternative. If you do this make sure that the kicker's team know that you are watching them by looking alternatively at them and the kicker as he prepares to take the kick.

No matter where you stand, go hard for the goal line as soon as the ball is kicked.

# LAW 28
## *Free Kick*

A free kick is a kick awarded for a fair-catch or to the non-offending team as stated in the Laws.

A goal shall not be scored from a free kick by the kicker unless the ball has been first played by another player.

For an infringement it may be taken by any player of the non-offending team.

It may be taken by any form of kick provided that the kicker, if holding the ball, must propel it out of his hands or, if the ball is on the ground, he must propel it a visible distance from the mark. He may keep his hand on the ball while kicking it.

1. The team awarded a free kick has the option of taking a scrummage at the mark and shall put in the ball.

2. When a kick is taken, it must be taken without undue delay.

3. The kick must be taken at or behind the mark on a line through the mark and the kicker may place the ball for a place kick.

4. If the place prescribed by the Laws for the award of a free kick is within five metres of the opponents' goal line, the mark for the free kick, or the scrummage taken instead of it, shall be five metres from the goal line on a line through that place.

5. The kicker may kick the ball in any direction and he may play the ball again without restriction.

6. The *kicker's team*, except a placer for a place kick, must be behind the ball until it has been kicked.

7. The *opposing team* must not wilfully resort to any action which may delay the taking of a free kick. This includes actions such as wilfully carrying, throwing, or kicking the ball away out of reach of the kicker.

8. The *opposing team* must retire without delay to or behind a line parallel to the goal lines and ten metres from the mark or to

their own goal line if nearer to the mark, or five metres from their opponents' goal line if the mark is in In-goal. Having so retired, players of the opposing team may charge with a view to preventing the kick, as soon as the ball has been placed on the ground or the kicker begins his run or offers to kick.

Retiring players will not be penalised if their failure to retire ten metres is due to the rapidity with which the kick has been taken, but they may not stop retiring and enter the game until an opponent carrying the ball has run five metres.

9.  If having charged fairly, players of the opposing team prevent the kick being taken, and do not gain advantage, the kick is void.

10.  Neither the kicker nor the placer shall wilfully do anything which may lead the opposing team to charge prematurely. If either does so, the charge shall not be disallowed.

**Penalty:**

— For an infringement by the *kicker's team* or for a void kick – a scrummage at the mark and the opposing team shall put in the ball.

If the mark is In-goal, the scrummage shall be awarded five metres from the goal line on a line through the mark.

— For an infringement by the *opposing team* – a free kick ten metres in front of the mark or five metres from the goal-line whichever is nearer on a line through the mark. Any player of the non-offending team may take the kick.

If the mark is In-goal, a drop-out shall be awarded.

## LAW 28

The first three paragraphs on the notes to Law 27 (Penalty kick) also apply to the free kick.

Let us look at some of the main differences between a free kick and penalty kick.

Bearing in mind that the player taking the kick may not kick directly for goal and that opponents may charge, referees should be alert to the options open to the kicking side, including a drop goal by one of the kicker's team-mates. The referee should not be in too great a hurry to sprint up-field to 'pose under the posts' if he can sense the possibility of the kick being charged down.

One of the most interesting recent law changes concerns the tap free kick where the kicker places the ball on the ground at or close to the mark. At this point the offending team may charge fairly and if they prevent the kick being taken, and do not gain advantage, the kick is void, and a scrummage is awarded with their put in. What would constitute an advantage in this situation? The obvious one is a member of the offending team who fly hacks the ball thirty to forty metres down field and the ball perhaps goes into touch: or if the team awarded the free kick are so dilatory that an opponent is allowed to pick the ball up and start a passing movement. If that is the case and no advantage accrues the good referee will award a scrum back at the mark of the free kick, with the side who conceded the free kick in the first place putting the ball in.

What of foul play by the offending team after the free kick has been awarded? In a penalty situation the penalty is advanced ten metres but in a free kick situation, the free kick is changed to a penalty at the original mark. If there is then further foul play, that penalty is then advanced ten metres.

If at a free kick taken quickly the offending side do not retire ten metres and they illegally stop the side taking the free kick then the free kick is advanced ten metres.

# GLOSSARY OF TERMS AND DEFINITIONS

ATTACKING TEAM: The opponents of the defending team.

BEYOND, BEHIND OR IN FRONT: Means that both feet of the player must comply.

BOUND: Binding onto a player with at least one arm. The definition of arm being from the shoulder to the wrist.

DEAD: This occurs when the referee blows his whistle to indicate a stoppage of play or when an attempt to convert a try is unsuccessful.

DEFENDING TEAM: The team in whose half of the ground a stoppage of play takes place.

DROP KICK: A drop kick is made by letting the ball fall from the hands (or hands) to the ground and kicking it at the first rebound as it rises.

FAIR CATCH or MARK: Awarded when a player being stationary, with both feet on the ground catches the ball from an opponent and at the same time shouts 'MARK'. Can only be awarded to a player within his own 22 metre or In-goal areas.

GOAL: Awarded when the ball is kicked over an opponent's crossbar from a penalty kick, conversion kick or drop kick.

IN-GOAL: The area bounded by the goal line, touch-in-goal line and dead-ball line.

KICK: A kick is made by propelling the ball with any part of the leg or foot (except the heel) from the knee to toe inclusive. If the player is holding the ball, he must propel it out of his hands. If the ball is placed on the ground, it must be propelled a visible distance.

KICK-OFF: A kick taken by a team at the centre of the pitch at the commencement the game, the commencement of the second half or after a try has been awarded.

KNOCK-ON: Occurs when a player loses possession of the ball and it goes forward and then strikes the ground or another player.

LINE THROUGH THE MARK OR PLACE: A line parallel to the touch line.

MARK: Place where a free kick or penalty kick is awarded.

MAUL: Occurs in the field of play when at least one player from each side is in physical contact around another player who is carrying the ball.

OFF-SIDE: Off-side is when a player is in a position under Law 24 in which he can not take part in the game.

ON-SIDE: A player is not off-side and can therefore take part in the game without penalty.

PENALTY TRY: Awarded by the referee if a try was prevented from being scored by foul play.

PLACE KICK: A place kick is made by kicking the ball after it has been placed on the ground, on sand or on a kicking tee.

PLAN OF FIELD AND ASSOCIATED TERMS: As contained in Law 1.

PUNT: A punt is made by letting the ball fall from the hand or hands and kicking it before it touches the ground.

REFEREE: Person appointed or mutually agreed to officiate at a match.

RUCK: Occurs in the field of play, when the ball is on the ground and at least one player from each side are on their feet and are bound onto each other.

SCRUMMAGE: Awarded after an infringement which does not warrant a penalty kick or free kick. A scrummage must have three players from each side in the front row and two players in the second row at all times. Binding of these players must conform to Law 20.

TACKLE: Occurs only in the field of play when a player carrying the ball is brought to the ground and is held on the ground by an opponent or opponents.

TOUCH JUDGE: The two people appointed or mutually agreed to assist the referee during the match.

TRY: Awarded when the ball is grounded by an attacking player in his opponents In-goal.

# Index